I0415245

The Chosen

Annette Gisby

The Chosen
©Annette Gisby 2013

ISBN: 978-1-291-50453-8

Cover art by Ravven
http://www.ravven.com

All Rights Reserved

No part of this book may be produced in any form, by photocopying
or by any electronic or mechanical means, including information
storage or retrieval systems, without permission in writing from both
the copyright owner and the publisher of this book, except for the
minimum words needed for review.

This is a work of fiction. All characters, incidents and places are
works of the author's imagination. Any resemblance to
real people, living or dead is purely coincidental.
Real locales, if used, are used in a fictional sense.

Prologue

Where was the bracelet? Xiana knew it had to be there somewhere. She'd put it at the bottom of her chest underneath her festival clothes, but it wasn't there. She frantically removed every item from the wooden chest, throwing them on the floor in her haste to search. Everything else was there, two jewelled combs, her spare linen shifts, five embroidered girdles, and three plain woollen gowns, her blue and red silks for festival days along with the white velvet cloak. But she could not find her precious bracelet.

Theft was almost unheard of in Sanctuary. The last incident had been over three hundred years ago, and the thief had been banished to the human realms. Why would anyone want to steal from her? There were other bracelets, other fripperies left in her chest, but they'd taken the one thing that was most precious to her.

It was precious to her because of what it symbolised. Eltan had given it to her that night—the night she became a woman. He had promised to return to wed her, and giving a bracelet was a betrothal custom of his people. She had believed him when he'd said he would return. Three moons had waxed and waned since then, still there was no sign of Eltan or of her moonblood. Xiana knew what that meant. Her father had tried to keep her sheltered, but even he couldn't prevent the other women from gossiping with her. She knew she was carrying Eltan's child.

She looked up at the sound of the slap of leather on the floorboards outside her doorway and met her father's angry face. With his white hair tied back in a warrior's braid, the lines on his face seemed so much more pronounced. There were rumours that his hair had turned white overnight when he'd lost his Firstwife, Xalia, Xiana's mother. His three Underwives had assumed that one of them would be elevated to the position of Firstwife, but Lyonada had been too grief-stricken and refused to elevate any one of them, or to take another Firstwife. The three Underwives took their frustrations out on Xiana when they were sure they could get away with it, but she could handle the beatings and chores. What she couldn't handle was her father's disappointment.

"Looking for this?" asked her father, fishing the bangle from the pocket of his tunic, which was white with two gold stripes down each side to signify that he was an Elder.

"Father! Where did you find it?"

"Who is he, Xiana? What human have you allowed to defile you so?"

"He hasn't defiled me," retorted Xiana, her face heating.

"No? Then Underwife Alia is lying, is she? You have not needed to attend the spring for the purifying ritual for the past three moons. How can you stand there denying your shame when I know you are carrying some vile human bastard within you?"

"Father, please! Let me explain. I love him, and he loves me. We're going to get married. He's coming back for me. He promised!"

"Coming back for you and taking you where? Out to the world of humans with their wars and disease? They almost destroyed us once, do you think we are going to stand by and let it happen again? I will never allow you to marry a human, never!"

"Father, please!"

"You're wasting your breath. It's the High Lord's decision now. You've broken the rules of Sanctuary. Now you must face the consequences of your actions. The child cannot stay here. Humans are not permitted in Sanctuary."

"It will be half-Aldari," protested Xiana.

"Half-Aldari is no Aldari at all. Come, the High Lord is waiting."

Chapter One

S old!" The slaver's voice rang out through the market square. "To the gentleman in the black cloak."

Severin pulled his hood closer around him despite the stifling heat. He must keep himself disguised at all costs. Oscians did not take kindly to strangers, and his icy blue eyes and silvery hair marked him a foreigner among the swarthy-skinned, dark-haired native population. Severin turned to his companion, a grey-haired man carrying the staff of a wizard. "Ildar, do we have enough gold?"

Ildar clucked his tongue. "It's a bit late to be worrying about that now, isn't it? You've already entered into the contract. Yes, we have enough, but only just. What's your father going to say when you bring home a slave?"

Severin smiled at his former tutor who was now one of his most trusted advisors. "Do you know me so little, Ildar?"

"You mean to set him free?"

"Of course. You know slavery is illegal in Arcathia. It's a pity we can't afford to free them all." Severin's eyes swept over the dais set up in the middle of the square where slaves of all ages stood or lay curled in their chains. Some were shackled to wooden stakes while others were bound to each other or had chains binding their arms and legs together so they could hardly move. Their tunics were stained, ill-fitting, and ragged around the hems, their arms and legs bare. Some held their heads high, yet others looked so despairing that Severin's heart lurched for them. He couldn't save them all, no matter how much he wanted to. Almost all of them were bruised and scarred in some way, testifying to abuse from previous owners or perhaps from the slave trader himself.

The slaver was a burly man with biceps the size of hams and thighs so thick they almost looked like tree trunks. He was bulging out of his leather jerkin and trousers. Sweat dripped down his face while he continued with the auction. Severin cringed. None of the scrawny slaves would have stood a chance against him if he decided to lay into them.

Severin looked at Ildar, raising his eyebrow in question. The two of them had known each other for so long that sometimes they didn't need words. Ildar nodded and cast a notice-me-not spell. It would shield them from prying eyes—there was no reason to make it easy for pickpockets. Once the shield was in place, Ildar counted out the requisite gold coins. He sighed every time he dropped a piece into Severin's open palm. "I hope we have enough left for lodgings for the night," said Ildar, his reluctance obvious.

"We could always camp out," said Severin. Ildar shuddered. For a wizard, he had a terrible aversion to nature and loved his home comforts. "Perhaps you should just conjure more gold pieces?"

Ildar gave a long-suffering sigh. "You see, this is why you were so hopeless at studying the Magical Arts. You can't conjure something from nothing. Magic is all about balance. It can only be used to assist nature. If you have a fire, you can make it warmer, but you can't conjure fire from thin air."

"I've heard the Aldari can do that and more."

"The Aldari? Well, if it's fairy tales you're after rather than reality, yes they can. But the Aldari have long since died out, and most of what is said about them is complete myth. They don't exist."

"So what about your spells? Like the notice-me-not? Isn't that something from nothing?"

"No, it uses my own magical energy and is cast on both of us, not into thin air. But I will not be able to cast another spell as strong as that until I've rested and had a good meal. Now, hadn't you better go pay for your young man?"

"He won't be mine for long. I'll set him free as soon as we're back in Arcathia." Severin knew there was no point in setting the slave free while they were still on Oscian soil. Runaway slaves were caught and if lucky only one leg was cut off, so they wouldn't try it again. Once punished they were sold to a master who didn't care that they were crippled. If unlucky, they were left out in cages for the crows until they died. The rotting carcasses remained in the open as a deterrent to others.

"Just make sure that you do," said Ildar, lowering his spell. Severin took the money up to the trader and handed it over. The slaver bit into each coin to make sure it was real before grunting something unintelligible to one of his helpers. A few moments later, someone thrust Severin's purchased slave before him. The slaver handed Severin his new owner's papers, and then waved them both away, intent on his next sale.

The youth seemed around Severin's age, or perhaps a bit younger, his face was clean shaven, but Severin couldn't tell if that was because he had indeed shaved or if it was because of his youth. The slave was short, barely reaching Severin's shoulder. Hair as dark as a raven's wing curled about a face so pale it was like looking at the moon. The boy stared at Severin, his violet eyes dull, almost as if unaware of what was going on around him.

Severin took the youth by the hand and led him back to Ildar. When he saw the welts that covered the youth's wrists and ankles, he felt sick. Some of them looked infected. Severin hoped Ildar had kept his herb store intact while they'd been travelling. It would take some time before they arrived in Arcathia and the boy could see a proper healer.

"I'm Severin and this is Wizard Ildar," he told the boy once they reached the wizard. "Do you have a name?"

"Havyn, Master Severin."

"Severin is fine. You don't have to call me Master."

"We'll have to stay in the town tonight," said Ildar, glancing at the sun sinking below the horizon. "There's no telling what sort of brigands might be on the road after dark."

"You're not very brave for a wizard," said the youth. He hunched over as if to protect himself from expected blows. Severin's heart ached for him. Vulnerability in others had always attracted him. He wanted to protect Havyn, to make sure the boy never suffered a fist raised in anger toward him ever again.

"It's foolishness to travel in the dark, not bravery," said Ildar, puffing out his chest in indignation.

"Come, we'll go find an inn, Ildar. I'm sure our budget can stretch to that, can't it?" Severin didn't know how much provision his father had made for them, but surely a stay at an inn for one night wouldn't leave them destitute, would it? The purpose of this journey had been to teach Severin about humility. For that reason, Ildar was in charge of the money.

"If we're frugal, don't order too much wine, and just have basic food. It will be cheaper if we sleep in the dormitories rather than a room to ourselves."

"I draw the line at that," said Severin. "Your snoring is bad enough. I don't want to hear twenty strangers too. We'll book a room, and if we have to, I'll forgo dinner this evening."

"On your own head be it." Ildar sighed as he waved the two of them ahead onto one of the side streets leading off the square.

The streets in Hammerfort were cramped and dirty. The buildings were so close to each other on their top storeys that it was almost like walking through a tunnel. Severin pulled his pack down from his shoulder and held out a pair of sandals to Havyn.

"What are you waiting for?" asked Ildar, leaning on his staff.

"He can't walk around in this filth in his bare feet." Unlike Arcathia, it seemed the citizens of Hammerfort hadn't yet discovered the wonders of indoor plumbing, and slop buckets fell from upper windows with alarming frequency.

Havyn looked at the sandals as if he'd never seen any item of footwear before. It took a while before he hesitantly reached out and accepted them, as if he wasn't sure that Severin wouldn't snatch them back and laugh in his face. The sandals weren't an exact fit, Havyn being much smaller, but they were better than nothing. Severin resolved that once they were home, he would organise fittings with the tailor and cobbler before he sent Havyn on his way in the world.

"This looks reasonably priced," said Ildar once they'd reached the end of the street furthest from the market square. A creaking sign above the grimy window proclaimed the place "The Smith's Arms", and indeed, a crudely drawn picture of two well muscled arms working a sword at an anvil hung above the door. An appalling stench emanating from the doorway almost bowled Severin over, but Ildar didn't seem to notice.

Drunken revellers spilled out onto the street, a few of them leering at Havyn, who moved closer to Severin and held onto his cloak. "No one will harm you," Severin promised, although looking at some of the toughs, he wondered if his own skill with a sword would be enough if they all decided to attack at once. One of the men vomited over the threshold of the inn, and then two of his friends dragged him off, all three of them singing off key as they staggered into the twilight.

The inn was crowded with people, some looked like smiths relaxing after their day's work, others had the look of soldiers or adventurers, yet others were apparently groups of travellers who looked warily at the door when Severin and his companions stepped carefully over the puddle of vomit. The smell made him a little nauseous himself, and he hurried the three of them over to the bar and the woman behind it.

Her face was caked with makeup, and her large bosom seemed in danger of falling out of the tight bodice that encased it. Havyn blushed, looking down at his feet. Had he never been in a tavern before?

"We'd like a room for three for the night," said Severin. "How much?"

"A gold piece for you and the wizard. The dog can sleep in the barn with the rest of the animals."

"We don't have a dog."

The alewife jerked a finger at Havyn. "Him."

"He's not a dog. He's a person!"

"He's a slave, ain't he? Slaves ain't people. He's an animal. I don't want my rooms fouled up."

"He will be staying with us. I insist," said Severin. "How much?"

"Oh, it's like that, is it?" the barmaid winked at him. "That'll be four gold pieces then. Food and drinks are extra."

"Do you have a bath house?"

She snorted. "A bath house? Oh of course, my lord." The woman made a mock curtsey. "And we have gold plated chamber pots an' all! Where do you think you are? In a palace? No, we ain't got a bath house, but I can send you up some hot water. There's a tub in the room. A fireplace too. Not every room has a fireplace, you know. That costs extra."

"Of course," said Severin, trying not to roll his eyes.

Ildar counted out the coins, tutting each time they left his hand, until finally, the woman seemed satisfied and issued them a large black key. "Room four, at the top of the stairs."

"Thank you."

'Room four' was an exaggeration 'broom cupboard four' might have been more apt. There was a large bed pushed up against one wall, while most of the other wall was taken up with a huge fireplace. The 'tub' was half of an ale barrel, which hardly looked watertight. A small table had one three-legged stool beside it, but there was no other seating in the room unless you counted the bed. One corner held a chipped chamber pot with a design of blue and white flowers.

"Do you think the bed has fleas?" asked Severin, looking askance at the filthy bedding.

"I can try a cleaning charm, but it's best if I do it after I've eaten." Ildar placed a hand on his ample belly as if just waiting for the food to arrive.

Someone knocked on the door as though they had just been waiting for Ildar to say he was hungry. Severin opened it to a boy and a girl of about ten summers old, who each carried two buckets of water. The buckets were almost as large as the children were. Ildar and Severin rushed to take the buckets from them and set them down on the hearth. The children waited, and didn't seem keen to leave.

The boy held out a grubby hand. Severin realised they wanted money. Ildar gave them each a silver penny, and they toddled off with gap-toothed grins.

"This is appalling. I've a good mind to report this establishment to the Taverners' Guild." Ildar's face turned purple. "First they give us a horrible room, and now they want money for all the extras!"

"Relax, Ildar. It's just for one night. Tomorrow we can make our way home. I'm sure my father has forgiven me by now."

"Indeed, I hope so."

Chapter Two

Havyn gasped when Master Severin removed his cloak. He had never seen hair of such a shade before. Severin's hair was so pale it was like looking at a cloud. It was long, almost to his waist and tied back at the nape of his neck with a black velvet ribbon. Severin's clothes were fancy, too—a black tunic with gold trim around the cuffs and hem. He also wore a pair of leather trousers and knee-length brown boots. Havyn had never worn boots. In fact, until today he had never worn any footwear at all. His heels had blistered where the strap of the sandal had rubbed against them while he walked, the sandals not being an exact fit.

"Havyn, you may bathe first, and then Ildar can put some salve on your injuries."

Havyn stared at his new Master. He was to be healed? No one had ever healed him before. Now that he thought about it, he couldn't remember a time when he hadn't been in some sort of pain. His last Master had made him lie on the floor beside his bed so that he could kick him during the night if he wanted to. Most nights, he had indeed wanted to.

"My clothes might be a little large for you, but they're clean. I have some towels here somewhere, too."

"Or I suppose we can always pay extra for them," grumbled Ildar. Havyn had not met many wizards, but of the few he had, none seemed as miserable as Ildar. Sometimes Havyn wished he'd been a wizard, maybe then he could have magicked himself away from all the horrible Masters he'd ever had. Master Severin didn't seem horrible. Havyn decided that he would just have to be so good that Severin would want to keep him. He wouldn't complain, he wouldn't argue, and he would work hard.

Severin pulled out a pair of soft doeskin breeches, a linen shirt with laces at the collar, and some underlinens, which he set on the bed. Rummaging in his pack again, he came up with two linen towels, which he hung on the rack next to the fireplace. Havyn stared at the clothes—real clothes, even underlinens! He'd never worn anything like them. Like most slaves in Oscia, he'd always been given a makeshift tunic, which was just sacking with holes cut out for his arms and head. The clothes on the bed looked so soft that Havyn wanted to reach out and touch them, but his hands were filthy, and he didn't want to soil them.

Severin turned and poured the water into the wooden tub one bucket at a time. While he was doing that, someone else came to the door with a small platter of black bread and pale cheese. Ildar stared at the serving lad and at the small portion of food. Even Havyn knew the wizard well enough by now to know that he wasn't impressed with having to fork out yet more coinage to the serving lad.

Havyn wondered why Severin wasn't handling the money, but then thought no more about it. Slaves had no business asking about money. Ildar was already seated at the table and digging into the bread when Severin had finished pouring the water.

"Ildar!" Severin scolded him. Was Severin angry because Ildar started eating before his Master? Severin seemed to be Ildar's Master, although Havyn didn't think the wizard was a slave. Some sort of servant, perhaps. "Let Havyn eat before his bath. He'll need his strength in order to heal properly."

Ildar stood up, flushed red. "I'm sorry, Severin, I didn't think. Here, Havyn, sit down. Get some food into you."

Sit down? On a stool? Like a real person? Tears gathered in the corner of his eyes, which made him even more determined to be a good slave for Master Severin. He sat gingerly on the stool and stared at the loaf of bread. Ildar had already carved a few slices off it and set them on the wooden platter. Havyn's mouth watered as he hesitantly lifted a slice of bread to his lips. The bread was hard and gritty, but it was the first food Havyn had eaten in weeks. Moaning around the bread, he had to stop himself from reaching for any more, afraid that his new master would be angry if he ate all the food. He risked a small piece of cheese before declaring himself full. "Thank you."

Severin arched an eyebrow at him, as if he couldn't quite believe that someone eating so little could indeed be full. "Right then. Time for your bath. Ildar and I will wait outside until you're finished."

"Don't get dressed yet," advised Ildar. "Just wrap the towel around you. I'll need to see your body to put the salve on."

"Yes, sir," said Havyn.

"Oh, I have some soap left in my pack. I notice that wasn't included in what we paid for."

While Ildar searched through his pack, Severin shared a conspiratorial wink with Havyn over Ildar's fussiness. Havyn stifled a giggle. When was the last time he had laughed? It was too long ago to remember. Ildar handed Havyn a small round ball, waxy to the touch. Havyn inhaled deeply of the scent, cinnamon and cloves.

Once Severin and Ildar left him alone to bathe, Havyn wasted no time in stripping off the reviled tunic—the emblem of his slavery. It didn't seem like Master Severin was going to want him to wear it again. Havyn took great delight in throwing it on the fire and watching the flames consume the hated garment. Havyn climbed into the tub. Although he was short, he still had to sit with his knees up against his chest in order to fit. The water was warm, and he couldn't resist the temptation of just sitting there for a few moments, enjoying the sensation. It was the first real bath he'd ever had. His previous Masters had just thrown buckets of cold water over him when they deemed him too filthy to be near them.

Havyn wet the ball of soap and rubbed it between his palms. He'd never used soap on himself before, but sometimes his Master or Mistress had wanted him to bathe them and he'd used it on them, so it wasn't as if he didn't know what to do with it. Ildar's soap made a soft, creamy lather and Havyn began by scrubbing his neck—the coarse edges of his tunic had always made his neck itch. His skin was rough with scabs and welts from all his previous abuses, but Havyn was beginning to hope that he'd found a Master who wouldn't mistreat him.

By the time he had finished washing, including soaping his hair, the water had turned a dingy gray, and Havyn felt guilty. He'd used up all the clean water, and Master Severin and Ildar still needed to bathe. Would Severin punish him for getting the water so dirty? Havyn stood on shaky legs. He dried himself with one of the linen towels. Once dry, he wrapped the other towel around his waist and went to open the door.

"I'm sorry," Havyn exclaimed when Severin and Ildar entered. "I didn't mean to make the water so dirty!"

"Havyn, calm yourself. The bath was for you. Ildar and I can wait a few days. We'll bathe when we get home. I doubt either of us would fit in that tub anyway." Severin laughed, and Havyn realised the man wasn't angry at all. "Ildar, have your meal. I'll rub the salve on Havyn. I don't need magic to do that, do I?"

"No, here." Ildar tossed a glass jar into Severin's hand. Severin surveyed Havyn's body, turning him this way and that. Havyn blushed under the scrutiny. He'd heard a few of the other slave boys talking about this sort of thing, some of them had been body slaves. Havyn wondered if that's what Master Severin wanted him for. Is that what the alewife had been hinting at when she'd winked at Severin when he'd insisted Havyn stay with them?

Havyn had never done anything like that before, none of his other Masters or Mistresses had expressed an interest in him. When they'd requested Havyn bathe them, that was all they'd requested of him. For some reason, Havyn had escaped that duty altogether, although some of the others he'd served with hadn't been that lucky. Some of them enjoyed it, but most did not.

"Hmm, the worst marks seem to be on your back," said Severin. "Are those scars from a whip?"

Havyn nodded, shame heating his cheeks. Whipping was the punishment reserved for the worst offenders, but half the time, his Masters had not told Havyn what he'd done wrong.

Severin removed the lid from the jar and spread some of the jelly-like substance on his fingers. "Hold out your wrists, Havyn. This will probably sting a bit."

Havyn gasped when the salve made contact with his sore wrists. It burned as if he had just dunked his hand into boiling water.

"Sorry," said Severin. "But it will help you to heal that much faster."

"Lie face down on the bed so I can do your back," suggested Severin once he'd finished with Havyn's wrists.

Havyn did what he was told. He clutched the pillow, filled with wonder even while he did so. He'd never been this close to a pillow before either. The bed dipped when Severin climbed onto it, straddling Havyn's hips. The weight, although an unusual sensation, was quite a pleasant one. He gasped at the first contact of the salve on his skin, his fingers tightening on the pillow. It was even worse than when Severin had put it on his wrists, Havyn bit his lip.

"I'll try to be gentler. I don't think I've inherited my mother's gift for healing."

"You're right there," said Ildar. "Yinare has a unique gift. It was a pity she never continued with her apprenticeship."

"Grandmother had other plans for my mother." Severin sighed. "And for me."

"You talk as if it was unusual. Every man must get married eventually, Severin. Especially you."

"I don't want to get married!" protested Severin, pressing down hard on Havyn's back.

"Ah!" Havyn groaned. He tried to arch away from the touch. It felt like Severin was taking out his frustrations on Havyn's skin.

"Sorry, Havyn. Ildar, eat your dinner. Let me do this in peace."

"You talk as if I was the one who brought the subject up," Ildar said and sniffed.

True to his word, Severin was indeed gentle this time, soothing the salve all over Havyn's back. Once the initial shock of the sting had worn off, the salve was quite pleasant. Severin's hands swept down from Havyn's neck to the small of his back, and then back up again. His fingers pressed the salve deep into Havyn's skin. The longer it went on, the more uncomfortable Havyn grew. So unused to any sort of touch that wasn't a punch or a blow, the light touch made him feel strange sensations in his chest and groin. He panted harshly into the pillow, not sure whether he was hoping Severin would stop soon or that he would continue doing this to him forever. "Havyn," Severin whispered, his hands slowly caressing Havyn's back.

Havyn shivered at the gentle touch, so different from any other he'd ever had. Severin may not have been a wizard like Ildar, but he must have magic hands to make Havyn feel so wonderful. Havyn closed his eyes. In his mind's eye, he saw Severin's hair spread out before him in the sky, and he lay upon it as if he was indeed floating on a cloud.

"No, no, no," ranted Ildar, snatching the jar from Severin's hand. "That's too gentle. The tissue will never heal if you don't knead it. Like this."

Havyn yelped when Ildar's rougher hands began to knead his skin like bread dough. The strange tension between himself and Severin evaporated instantly. Severin climbed down from the bed, and Havyn already missed the firm weight atop him. He had felt safe and protected, something completely foreign to him.

Havyn turned his head on the pillow and watched Severin standing by the fire. Severin's face was as flushed as Havyn knew his own to be. Havyn was hot, and he knew it had nothing do to with the fire. He stole another glance at Severin, suspicious that the pink stain on Severin's face had very little to do with the roaring flames either.

Chapter Three

Severin insisted that he would take the floor while Havyn and Ildar shared the bed that evening.

"Severin! You can't sleep on the floor," protested Ildar. "What would your father say?"

"Havyn is injured, and you are a not a young man anymore, Ildar," said Severin. "I'm healthy. I can manage the floor for one night."

"Master Severin, I can sleep on the floor," said Havyn. "I don't hurt much anymore."

"No, Havyn, you will rest in the bed. And stop calling me Master!"

Severin turned away from the violet-eyed gaze, but not before he saw the tears. Damn his angry tone. He hadn't meant to upset the youth, but then what was Havyn supposed to think? One minute Severin had been massaging him, the next shouting at him. Severin couldn't fathom his own behaviour, so how could he expect Havyn to feel? Severin's stomach tied itself in knots as he tried to work it out. Why did this youth affect him so? His head throbbed and his chest ached.

"Severin! What's gotten into you?"

"Nothing, Ildar, I'm just tired."

"All the more reason for you to sleep in the bed then," said Ildar, as if that settled the matter.

"I said no!" Severin yanked his cloak from the peg and wrapped it around himself. He settled onto the stool by the fireside. Maybe he was exhausted, but Severin knew there was no way he could sleep anyway. Why couldn't Ildar just leave him be? Why couldn't both of them?

"Is this about your father?" Ildar asked gently.

"No. Not everything in my life has to do with him."

"What is it then? You used to confide in me, Severin."

Severin swallowed several times, trying get rid of the lump in his throat, but the words refused to come. How could he explain this to

Ildar? Ildar was of the old school. He held that wizards lost their power if they lost their virginity, and Ildar had never taken a lover. Neither had Severin for that matter, but it was something he had often thought of and dreamt about. How could he talk to Ildar about anything related to that? How could he tell Ildar what had happened to him while putting the salve on Havyn's back? Severin turned to see Havyn's eyes on him once again. He pulled his cloak tighter around his body to hide his erection. Severin had to turn away.

"What side would you like, Havyn?"

"Here's fine," said Havyn, sounding very subdued. Severin wished he could, in fact, sleep on the bed with Havyn so that he could wrap him in his arms and comfort him. Severin dug his hands into his thighs. He may as well be honest in his own mind. He wanted to offer a lot more than comfort. Severin knew he was not like the Oscians who used others for their pleasure, whether willing or not. It would have to be a mutual thing. Had he imagined Havyn's reaction to his touch, or was Havyn feeling something for him too? Severin didn't know, and he didn't know how to bring it up either, not with Ildar hovering over them like a hen fussing over her chicks. Ildar wouldn't allow anything untoward to happen, not while he was chaperoning. The problem was that Severin wasn't even sure what it was he wanted to do with Havyn. He may have been a little bit older, but he wasn't well versed in any of the arts of love.

When he heard Ildar's snores, Severin looked across at the bed to see Havyn on the side of the bed nearest to him, his knees tucked up against his chin, his arms wrapped around them. The young man was fast asleep, the firelight dancing over his cheeks while he breathed in and out. Severin resisted the urge to go over and caress the pale skin. Havyn was dark-haired like the other Oscians, but Severin had never seen skin so pale on any Oscian before. Perhaps Havyn had been stolen from some other land and sold into slavery in Oscia. That wouldn't have been unusual.

Frustrated at looking, but unable to touch, Severin finally fell into a fitful sleep. His dreams were filled with the haunts of his earlier youth—the stables, fishing by the river, and boar hunting in the forest. But this time, his dreams were different. In all of them, unlike those of his youth, he had a laughing, violet-eyed companion by his side as they did all those things. In the dream, Severin pulled Havyn down onto the grass while they kissed each other breathless. Severin jerked awake. The front of his breeches was a sticky mess.

Checking that the others were still asleep, Severin pushed off his cloak and searched through his pack for some fresh underlinens and breeches. He washed his groin using the water left over from Havyn's bath, hoping this time, Ildar wouldn't comment on his dreams. Ildar was of the opinion that if a man spilled his seed in his sleep, it was because a demon was trying to suck out his soul. Severin had never heard any of the temple priestesses mention demons at all. Seeing that the others were still asleep, Severin used the chamber pot and cast a shaving spell on his face. It was the only magic he could do. He sat back down on the stool to wait for the others to wake.

With no windows, he had no idea when it might be morning, but after a time he could hear hustle and bustle from the rooms below. He guessed it would soon be time to leave. On the bed, Havyn yawned and stretched like a cat. His toes curled when he did so and Severin had to tear his eyes away. Havyn was exquisite. Severin had never seen such beauty on a male before. He'd seen plenty of handsome men, but he'd never seen one he would have considered beautiful.

Once Ildar was awake, all three of them shared the meagre remains of the bread and cheese from the previous evening. Time had done little to improve the fare, but at least it filled their bellies and they wouldn't have to start their journey on empty stomachs.

"Havyn, let me resize those clothes to fit you," said Ildar after he'd eaten. "The sandals first. It will be a lot easier for you to walk if they fit properly."

"Thank you," said Havyn, leaning down to undo the straps. Severin noticed how thin his ankles were. Havyn was thin all round. Did his previous owners starve him? Severin's stomach hurt at the idea of having eaten so much when they broke their fast. Guilt over the way Havyn had been starved ate away at him. He should have left a larger portion for the thin boy.

"No, leave them on. Then they will resize to your feet."

"Oh," said Havyn, nodding at the wizard and setting his hands on the table. The welts on his wrists looked a lot less angry today. Severin guessed Ildar's salve had been working its magic overnight. Ildar raised his hands and waved them around in front of Havyn's body saying some unintelligible words. Severin knew that Ildar had no need for all the theatrics. All a wizard needed to do was to think of the spell he needed and it happened. But people seemed to expect wizards to wave their hands or staffs about and say magic words in order for it to work. The air in front of Havyn shimmered gold for a moment or two. When it became clear again, Havyn glanced down at the clothes, which now fit him perfectly.

"*Oh!* No one has ever done magic on me before. Can anyone do magic?"

"All of us have some inherent magic," said Ildar. "But only certain people have a true affinity with it. Some try, but never master it."

"Shall we go?" asked Severin sullenly. He didn't want to be reminded of his own failures in trying to master magic. "The sooner we get started, the sooner we can get there."

"So keen to see your father again?" asked Ildar with a taunting smile.

"Maybe he'll have had time to miss me," said Severin, although in truth, he thought his father would have been pleased to be rid of him for a while longer. When they made their way down the stairs, the alewife of the establishment cornered them by the doorway. "You still owe two gold pieces," she said, her hand out, ready for them.

"For what?" demanded Ildar. "We've paid enough!"

"You haven't paid the tax."

"What tax?"

"The Taverners' Guild tax. Two gold pieces a night for every night you spend in an inn in Hammerfort."

"This is outrageous! Daylight robbery!"

"Ildar, just pay her so we can go."

Ildar huffed, paying the tax with bad grace. Severin, for his part, was just glad to get out of the place and into the fresh air. Well, the air at least. The town of Hammerfort smelled more like an abattoir or a midden heap rather than the fresh, flowery scents of home. They'd been away long enough.

Two bored-looking soldiers stopped them at the town gate. It was an annoyance because they were two who just wanted to feel important, or at least that's the impression they gave Severin. "Papers," demanded the taller of the two guards. Beneath the ragged beard, the man's top two front teeth were missing. Severin removed the papers from his pack, smiling with confidence. The false papers had passed inspection before and there was no doubt in his mind that they would again.

The guard looked at the parchments while Severin held his breath. "He's a slave, why isn't he wearing a tunic?" the bearded man asked, nodding toward Havyn.

"I was under the impression that once a slave was purchased it was up to the new owner to decide what clothes their slave could or couldn't wear."

"That's true," the guard admitted. "But most Oscians allow nothing but the tunics so they can know instantly who's a slave or who isn't. Dressed like that, he could almost be mistaken for normal folk."

"We're not Oscian," said Severin, trying to rein in his temper.

"Obviously," drawled the guard. "You're as beardless as girls." In Arcathia, anyone with a beard would have looked suspicious. If they were hiding their face, what else were they trying to hide? For the Oscians, the hairier a man looked the more he was revered as a great warrior. Just another thing their two nations never agreed on.

"On your way, then," said the guard, returning the papers and waving them through the gate. There were few other people on the road in the early hours, but Severin was glad of the timely start. The day would soon heat up, and he wanted to travel a good distance before that happened.

"How far is it to Arcathia?" Havyn asked while the three of them trekked along the dusty path between the trees.

"About five days' march," replied Severin, adding another day onto the estimate to take into consideration Havyn's slower pace. Not that he begrudged the boy a slower walk. Havyn still wasn't healed from his wounds.

"Why don't you just use a portal stone?"

Ildar laughed. "Oh, you two are a pair. First Severin thinks the Aldari still exist and now you think portal stones do."

"What are portal stones?" asked Severin.

"What are Aldari?" asked Havyn at the same time.

Ildar rested his arm on the top of his staff. "Well now, Havyn. You're in for a tale. Let's find some shade, and I can tell you a tale of the Aldari."

They left the road and took shelter beneath an oak tree. The ground around it was littered with acorns. Ildar sank down, his back to the trunk of the tree. Havyn and Severin sat cross-legged in front of him, both of them rested their chins on their hands.

"The Aldari were once called the Chosen or the Guardians. There was a great battle thousands of years ago between the human world and the demon world. The gods created the Aldari to help us and to protect us from the demons. Once the demons were defeated, some humans did not believe that victory was due to the Aldari. In fact, some began to see the Aldari themselves as demons. They were hunted and killed, all but dying out. To save some semblance of their race, they left the human world for a magical realm that no one but they can enter. Although there have been tales of humans falling through accidentally. According to legend, the Aldari could do many things. They could summon fire and water at will, they were also considered to be shape shifters—they could change their shape into anything they desired, an animal, another person, even change their sex. But the only remains of the Aldari today are wizards. It was the Aldari who gave the human race its magical abilities."

"How?" asked Havyn.

"Their bloodlines. Some Aldari took human lovers, and their children were magical, like the Aldari. Today, anyone who is a wizard has to have at least one Aldari ancestor."

"And portal stones?" asked Severin.

"Legend has it that the Aldari could make a stone into a portal so they could travel great distances in almost an instant. They just had to think of where they wanted to go. Not just any stone though, it had to be a fossilised dragon egg."

"But dragons don't exist, do they?" asked Severin.

"Well no, that's why it's considered a myth," said Ildar. "It would be wonderful though, wouldn't it? To be able to go where you wanted in an instant! No more camping, no more walking."

"But I've used one," said Havyn softly.

"What?" Ildar's head whipped around, and he stared at the youth.

"A portal stone. One of my other Masters was a wizard. We used the stone to travel."

"You did?" asked Ildar. "How often?"

"Just the once. They can only be used once."

Ildar nodded. "That was also considered part of the legend. There was only enough power in the stone for it to be used once. So, you have indeed seen portal stones, Havyn? You're not making it up?"

Severin could almost feel the air around Havyn crackle with energy. "I may be a slave but I have honour. I don't lie!" Havyn stood, brushed his breeches free of grass and dust before running off. Ildar and Severin exchanged wary glances.

"Go after him," urged Ildar.

"Havyn," Severin called. "Havyn! Wait!"

Chapter Four

"Havyn! Wait!" Severin called again. Havyn kept walking, his head down. He had been foolish to assume that perhaps Severin thought of him as anything other than a slave. Foolish to hope. Now he'd spoken out against his Master too. He had been taught better than that. Havyn sank to the ground, touching the grass with his forehead and his hands.

"Forgive this unworthy slave, Master," said Havyn.

"Havyn, please get up," said Severin. "You don't understand."

Havyn lifted his head, but didn't stand up. He knew his place. Slaves who spoke out against their master deserved to be punished. Severin sat down on the grass next to him.

"Havyn, you aren't a slave. I bought you so that we could free you. I wish we could have freed all of you, but even I don't have enough gold for that."

"Free me?" Havyn had dreamed of just that so often. Imagined that he'd be free to do whatever he wanted with no Master to take orders from. That he'd suffer no more beatings when he did things wrong. It would be heaven to have food whenever he wanted and a real bed to sleep in. But a dream was all it was. Freedom would mean little to him. Havyn had no money, no skills. Freedom wouldn't improve his life. He'd end up begging on the streets or worse. At least as a household slave he'd always had a roof over his head. "But I have nowhere to go."

"We'll work something out," said Severin.

"Why—why did you choose me? There were lots of slaves at the auction."

"Havyn, I..." Whatever else Severin had been about to say was interrupted when Ildar approached them, out of breath and clutching his side from that little exertion.

"You are not what you seem," Havyn whispered to Severin when Ildar came nearer.

"Well, boys, have you made up? Shall we continue on?"

"Ildar, I think we may have found you a new apprentice." Severin smiled. "Havyn senses I may not be what I seem."

"Oh? Indeed? You're a Seeker, Havyn? What other magic can you do?"

"It's not magic. It's just something I've always been able to do—to sense when people are lying."

"Indeed. A Truth Seeker. Well, when we get back to the palace, I can help teach you. Is that something you'd be interested in doing?"

"You mean I could become a wizard?" asked Havyn. His head spun and butterflies fluttered in his stomach. This was so unexpected. He swallowed the lump in his throat and tried to stop the tears, but they flowed anyway.

"My dear, Havyn, you are already a wizard, I would just help you hone your skills and powers. I have been looking for an apprentice for years. This is quite a stroke of luck for both of us. We can discuss it further when we get home."

"Home is a palace?"

Ildar grinned. "Oh, yes. Allow me to introduce Prince Severin of Arcathia."

* * * *

Each night before they camped, Ildar put more salve on Havyn's wounds, and Havyn missed Severin's gentler touches. Ildar was rough with him, but as the days went by, Havyn noticed that his skin was improving. Soon it was as if he'd never been injured at all.

They took turns on watch each night because Ildar was still wary about attacks by brigands, not to mention sleeping out in the open. Ildar was always grumbling about something, but rather than annoying, Havyn found it quite endearing. There was no malice in Ildar's complaints. In fact, it seemed as if he enjoyed complaining. Havyn soon learned not to worry much about what he said. Havyn had no trouble sleeping on the ground. A slave took his rest where he could.

During Havyn's turns at watch, he found himself staring at Severin, his mind reeling. Severin was a prince! Havyn had known there was something more to the man as soon as he'd seen him. Havyn hadn't been wrong. He'd always been able to sense things about people. Even before he was bought by certain Masters, he knew which of them would mistreat him and which wouldn't. But it wasn't as if he could ask the slave trader to sell him only to the ones who weren't going to beat him. The trader would have sold him to the highest bidder regardless.

Havyn could hardly believe his luck. A prince had bought him, and now a wizard wanted to train him as an apprentice! It was like something out of a tale, and he wondered if he was dreaming all of this. Such good things never happened to him, but if the gods willed it, he was not going to complain.

When the fire died to glowing embers, Ildar awoke and stretched, almost as if he knew when it was his turn to take watch.

"Ohhh, my back," Ildar groaned, rubbing the base of his spine with both hands. "It'll be so good to get back to my own bed. You get some rest, Havyn. It's another early start in the morning. We want to get home."

"Yes, sir," said Havyn. He snuggled down a few paces away from Severin. He'd just laid down when Severin shook him awake. Havyn sat up and rubbed his eyes free of sleep. The three of them shared a breakfast of wild mushrooms and bread cooked over the fire. Once they'd finished, Severin poured water over the flames and packed everything up.

"Ready, Havyn?" asked Severin. Ildar, already wearing his pack, leaned impatiently on his staff, obviously eager to get home.

Havyn's heart thudded with excitement. He'd never seen a palace, and hoped he wouldn't make a fool of himself.

"Ready," said Havyn with a smile at his Master.

* * * *

Arcathia's capital city glittered in the sunlight. The streets were broad and lined with pretty whitewashed houses with red tiled roofs. In the gardens, profusions of colourful flowers nestled side by side with vegetables. Some of the houses were hidden behind marble walls, but Havyn heard the trickle of water from behind them. He guessed there might be fountains or ponds. It was a luxury unheard of in Oscia where water was so scarce that it had never been used for anything decorative like a fountain.

Horses and carriages rode by, but the streets were immaculate. There was no worry of stepping into any filth here. Severin and Ildar quickened their pace along a tree lined avenue, and Havyn had to run to keep up with them. He guessed they must be nearing the palace, and his mouth went dry.

What if the king and queen didn't like him? Would they make Severin sell him? Havyn wasn't sure if he believed Severin about being free. Maybe slaves couldn't train as wizarding apprentices. Perhaps Severin would free him so Ildar could train him. What happened after that though? Would he still belong to Severin? Or would he then be expected to make his own way as a wizard? It was a daunting thought.

"Welcome to the White Palace," said Severin when they reached the brow of the hill.

Havyn stood, gaping at the vision before him. The palace was as large as a city by itself. There were turrets flying white pennants with the image of a black raven on them. There were also red ones with a golden sword. Havyn saw other flags too, but couldn't make out the devices on them. Every inch of the castle had the appearance of white marble, but once they got closer, Havyn could see the palest trace of grey veins running through it.

At the large wrought iron gates, they were stopped by two guards who crossed two lances in front of them.

"Halt! Who goes there?"

"Chayal, is that any way to greet your prince?" growled Ildar, glaring at the guard.

"By the Raven! It is you." Chayal and the other guard sank to one knee, bowing their heads, the sun glinting off their metal helmets.

"Get up, you two," said Severin. "You know I hate all that."

The guards got up and grinned at the party. "Kelandra's going to kill you, you know that, right?" asked Chayal.

"What are you on about now, Chayal?" said a female voice from behind them. The woman had dark auburn hair done in two braids hanging down over her chest. On seeing the three of them beyond the guards, she stopped dead in her tracks and just stared. Unlike any other woman Havyn had ever seen, she wasn't wearing a gown, but wore a pair of breeches and an over tunic like the guards. Whereas their tunic was white with the black raven, hers was red with a golden sword on it. A sword hung from her left hip in a leather scabbard.

"Hello, Kelandra." Severin bowed from the waist.

"Don't you 'hello Kelandra' me!" she snarled, her hands on her hips. "What got into you? You were supposed to wait for me before you went on your journey. Running off like that without your guards. It's a wonder you weren't killed! Your father blames me for not going with you. He didn't want you to go without a guard."

"You were just there," said Severin. "You know it's me he's angry with."

"Kelandra, let me introduce Havyn. He is to become my new apprentice," said Ildar. Kelandra looked at Havyn and smiled.

"Forgive my bad manners, Havyn. Be welcome in Arcathia." She crossed both arms over her chest and bowed to him. Havyn stared. No one had ever bowed to him before.

"Pleased to meet you, Princess Kelandra," said Havyn, returning the same gesture. From the way she and Severin talked to each other, Havyn guessed they were brother and sister.

Kelandra laughed. "Oh, I'm no princess, Havyn."

"Kelandra is a Daughter of the Sword," said Ildar. "She's one of Prince Severin's bodyguards."

"A *girl* bodyguard?" blurted Havyn before he could stop himself.

She laughed again. "Indeed, Havyn. You have a lot to learn about Arcathia."

"Kelandra, can you take Havyn to my mother? He was injured and may need some more tending," said Severin. "I had better face my father."

"Of course. This way, Havyn. We'll get you settled in before dinner. Queen Yinare will soon have you patched up."

"Thank you," Havyn said, taking her outstretched hand.

"Good luck," Kelandra called back to Severin.

"I'll need it," said Severin as he and Ildar took off in a different direction.

"So, Havyn. You're a wizard, then?" Kelandra asked him while they made their way through a maze of avenues.

"Ildar seems to think so. I never knew what I could do was considered magic. I just did it."

She stopped by a large wooden door, the frame carved with flowers and animals, and knocked on it. A few moments later, a woman draped in a shimmering gold gown emerged. Her blond hair hung loose and was wreathed in flowers. She was a lot younger than Havyn had expected the queen to be.

"Lady Kessarie, we'd like to see Queen Yinare," said Kelandra through gritted teeth. Havyn didn't need any magical sense to know these two women got on as well as oil and water. Kessarie stared at Havyn, making him uneasy. There was such darkness within her, it made his chest ache.

"She's resting," said Kessarie, her hands on her hips, blocking the doorway.

"We're here at Prince Severin's request," said Kelandra.

"He's back?" The woman flushed. "When?"

"Just now. He's gone to see his father."

"So he won't be able to see his mother yet anyway. Come in. But don't touch anything," said Kessarie, looking askance at Havyn as if she suspected him of being some sort of petty thief. Havyn may have been a slave, but he still had honour. Never in his life had he stolen anything, even when he was so hungry death might have been preferable.

"Wait here," said Kessarie, leading them to a room filled with couches and cushions in soft jewel tones. Kessarie went through an inner doorway, Havyn presumed to let the queen know they were there. Plinths in each corner of the room held vases or sculpted busts of people. Latticed windows overlooked a courtyard with a pool covered in water lilies and a fountain in the middle of it.

A few moments later, a woman with long grey hair, wearing a pale blue gown, emerged from a hidden doorway beside Kessarie. The woman smiled at them. "Kelandra, my dear. Kessarie informs me my wayward son has returned?"

"Yes, your majesty," said Kelandra, curtseying.

"Now, none of that. I'm in my private quarters. And here, I'm Yinare, not the queen. Now then, who's this?"

"Havyn is Ildar's new apprentice," said Kelandra. Havyn bowed like Severin had done. "He needs healing."

"I see. Well, Havyn, come with me. They tell me I have a gift for healing, so you're in safe hands."

Kessarie glowered at Kelandra, then at him, and Havyn wasn't so sure of her.

Chapter Five

After discovering that his father wasn't in his apartments, Severin dumped his pack in his own bedroom and headed off to the mews. Like he'd expected, his father was there with the falconer, expressing concern over one of his hawks. Those birds got more of his father's attention than Severin had ever received. It was as if once his Queen had given him an heir, King Faran wanted nothing more to do with either of them. Growing up, Severin had spent more time in the women's apartments than with his father.

It was Chayal who had taught Severin to hunt and how to use all the weapons he was supposed to be able to master. Ildar tutored him in all of the other academic subjects, including magic, but Severin had very little talent for that. It was something he knew disappointed his mother. Perhaps it had disappointed his father also, but since to Faran, Severin was a complete disappointment, it mattered little.

Faran had wanted a warrior for a son, not a scholar. Ill-health during his childhood had made his heart weak, and Severin knew the warrior's life was not for him. It hadn't mattered to Faran. He made sure Chayal tested Severin to his limits, and sometimes, Severin was sure he saw his father watching their practices from one of the palace windows.

"So. You've returned," said Faran. "No apology?"

"I have nothing to apologise for, Father," said Severin, his hands clenched into fists by his sides.

"No? You turn down the best offer of marriage you'll ever have and you say you have nothing to be sorry for?"

"I don't want to get married!" protested Severin. "I already told you that."

"You're twenty-one years old, and the only heir to the Arcathian throne! What happens when I'm gone and you're left a bachelor? There'll be bloodshed if you don't sire a son and soon. Do you want to bring us back to the brink of civil war? That's what it will come down to. Leave us," Faran commanded the falconer. The man bowed and hastily made his retreat, the birds squawked when he did so.

"Chayal told me what happened at your initiation," said Faran in a much gentler tone. "That you were not pleased by any of the eligible women. There is no shame in it for them or for you, Severin. The prince's first chosen is an honour and one not lightly bestowed. But why didn't you go through with it?"

Severin blushed, and mentally made a note never to speak to Chayal again. The man was supposed to be his friend. Then he realised that being the head of the Raven Brotherhood, Chayal's first loyalties were to his king. They were his father's bodyguards, not his.

"Have you lain with anyone at all? Perhaps you preferred to keep it private between the two of you?"

"No, Father. No one." Heat crept into his cheeks as he spoke.

"But don't you see? This is even better. Anyone offering for you will have to offer a much higher dowry since you're a virgin, which is unusual for Arcathian males. You could have your pick of princesses," said Faran, trying to coax him.

Why couldn't his father understand? Severin didn't want his pick of princesses. The idea of lying with a woman didn't interest him. He didn't dislike women, in fact, Kelandra was one of his best friends, but the thought of being intimate like that with any of them wasn't something he had ever wanted.

"Father, I am not interested in princesses, or any other women," said Severin wondering how to tell his father what he really wanted. Severin took a deep breath and just decided to come right out with it. He was already a disappointment to his father, what was one more? "I don't want to get married, Father. I am not interested in women like that. I'm interested in men."

Much to his surprise, the king laughed. "Severin, of course I know you're not interested in women in that way. I've seen the way you look at the guards when they are practicing. You've never even looked at the Daughters like that. It doesn't matter. You're a royal prince. You have responsibilities to the kingdom. Marriage is the only way to get a legitimate heir. It must be done. Take a male lover if you wish, but you must get married. I knew you would never agree, no matter how many offers came your way, so I have arranged for us to go to Oscia in two weeks time to arrange a betrothal to Princess Ythrin."

"Oscia! Are you mad? The Oscians hate us. And they keep slaves! Who is Ythrin? King Eltan doesn't have any children."

"That's true. Princess Ythrin is his niece, his brother's child. He adopted her when her parents died. Like Arcathia, Oscia can only have a male ruler. Once you married her, you would become King of both Oscia and Arcathia. A joint kingdom. Imagine the good you could do, Severin. You could abolish the slave trade in Oscia, you would be their king."

"King Eltan has agreed to this match, has he? What about all the bad blood between our nations?"

"Severin, Eltan and I are getting on in years. Neither of us expects to live forever. We want to form a truce and put the past behind us. This is a good thing, for both our nations. Surely you can see the sense in it?"

Unfortunately, Severin could indeed see the sense in it. Oscia and Arcathia had not been at war with each other for a few years, but by turning down the marriage proposal, Severin could well set them on that violent course again. There had been tentative peace between them for three years, was Severin going to just throw all that away? He was a prince, as his father had said, he had responsibilities. Marriage for him wasn't about love, but about political alliances. This would be the best match for both of their kingdoms.

"How does Ythrin feel about marrying me?"

"She will do her duty, as will you."

Severin tried not to roll his eyes. Of course, as a princess, she probably had not been asked about what she would like in a husband. Severin suspected that Ythrin had been brought up with little thought for love, just like him. It was all about politics.

"You should bathe, and then go see your mother. She has missed you," said Faran. He turned away to pet one of the smaller falcons. There were no embraces for Severin.

"Very well, Father," said Severin. There was nothing more to be said.

* * * *

Havyn didn't know how long he'd been asleep. After Queen Yinare had tended to the last of his wounds, she'd given him a drink, and the next thing he knew, it was dark outside when he woke. There were two candles alight on a table by the bed casting flickering shadows on the gilded ceiling. Havyn struggled to push himself upright. His limbs were so difficult to control; they felt as if they belonged to someone else. He strained to hear voices in another room. His hearing had always been good, no matter how many clips around the ear he'd gotten from his previous Masters.

"How is he?" Havyn's heart rate increased at the sound of Severin's voice. He couldn't believe the prince was asking after him.

"He will be fine, Severin. I've given him a sleeping draught so he can rest. A few decent meals in him wouldn't go astray either. The poor boy is skin and bone. So it's true, then? They really do keep slaves in Oscia?"

There was no reply, but Havyn guessed Severin might have nodded.

"I see," replied Yinare. "I thought it was just a rumour to make Oscians seem more like monsters so we'd feel more comfortable going to war with them. Like they think we eat our children. Have you seen your father?"

"Yes. We're going back to Oscia in two weeks to arrange the betrothal."

"You've agreed to marry her?" Yinare asked, sounding surprised.

"What else can I do, Mother? It's my duty, isn't it? The kingdom needs an heir."

"Oh, Severin. You're a good boy. Any mother would be proud of you, but I know how much you are giving up to do this."

"No more than you had to," said Severin. "Your wedding wasn't a love match, was it?"

"Severin, we agreed not to discuss that. Did you know your friend Havyn is a seeker?"

"He told us he could sense things about people, when they were lying or hiding something. I've never known one before."

"It's quite a rare gift, even among wizards. His Aldari ancestry must be very close. Havyn must be only a second or third generation."

"Ildar is convinced that the Aldari no longer exist."

"Much as I like Ildar, Severin, on this, he is wrong. You were too young to remember King Eltan's bride, she was a pure-blooded Aldari called Xiana. We were friends for a time. She and both her children died during childbirth. That's what started the most recent war between our nations. Eltan was convinced she had been murdered by an Arcathian."

"Had she?"

"No. It was a great tragedy, but the poor man was mad with grief. He wanted someone to blame, needed someone to blame. Eltan has never recovered from that. Eltan loved his wife and vowed never to marry again. He wanted no one to take her place, even though he had no living children."

"So no heir. How did his brother die? Father said he adopted his niece."

"Severin, you don't want to hear that story. Not if there is going to be peace between our nations."

"Mother, please, I need to know. I need to know what to expect."

Havyn already knew the story, everyone in Oscia did, it was still the subject of gossip even these many years later, but he guessed it would shock Severin, who to Havyn, seemed to be of a very delicate constitution.

"I told you, King Eltan went mad with grief over the loss of his wife and children. He banned all marriage in Oscia and forbade men and women to have any contact with each other. He ordered the execution of anyone who got married as well as that of any children born of their union. "

"No!" Severin cried, sounding horrified.

"His brother eloped, but somehow, Eltan found out. He and his wife were executed, but Eltan allowed the child to live, a daughter, Princess Ythrin."

"Eltan killed his own brother? And Father expects me to marry into that family?"

"The fact that Eltan has approached us concerning marriage to Ythrin shows that he, too, wants to put the past behind him and forge an alliance."

"Or it's a trap," said Severin. "Have me marry Ythrin so then he can murder both of us."

"What would be the sense in that?"

"I don't know, but you said yourself he was mad. Maybe he still is."

"I don't think so, Severin. The man is dying, he needs this marriage."

"I still think it might be a trap," said Severin.

"That's why you are taking Havyn with you. He'll know if Eltan is telling the truth or not."

Havyn's hands clutched at the bedclothes. He thought he had escaped Oscia forever. The fact that he would soon be going back to help arrange Severin's betrothal made it seem so much worse.

Havyn blinked back tears, choked back his sobs, and lay back on the pillows, completely devastated.

Chapter Six

Havyn stood on a platform in the middle of his bedroom while the tailor and Master Severin discussed what colours and styles of attire might suit him. Havyn stood nervously while both Severin and the tailor looked him up and down. He wasn't used to standing around in his underlinens. It was all he could do not to cover his chest with his arms, although not so much to hide the scars anymore. With both Ildar and Queen Yinare's care, most of Havyn's scars had faded to mere white marks on his skin, and none of them hurt anymore. No, it was Severin's scrutiny he wanted to hide from.

Havyn never had the luxury of his own bedroom before. For the first few nights, in the quarters he'd shared with Ildar, he had slept on the floor, not quite sure that the wizard meant for him to sleep on the bed. Havyn thought it might be some sort of test to see if he would dare to do such a thing, but Ildar had discovered him sleeping on the floor and insisted that yes, the bed was Havyn's and he wouldn't need to sleep on the floor.

The bedroom floor was tiled with a black and white mosaic design of birds and other animals, and the walls whitewashed. Curtains in shimmering jewel tones of emerald, amethyst, sapphire, silver, and gold fell in folds from the ceiling to envelop the bed. Cushions matching the curtains were piled high among the pillows. Two tables at either side of the bed held unlit glass covered candles. The sunlight flooded through the open shutters, giving enough light to the room. At night, the latticed shutters could be pulled across, but their open fretwork design allowed air to flow into the room and offset the heat of the day. From his bedroom window, he had a view of the harbour along with all the boats moored there or sailing in and out. He wondered what it would be like to sail to new and exotic lands, but didn't dwell on it.

In addition to the bedroom, there was a private bathroom. It was some sort of magical one, for instead of having to lug buckets to fill the bath, there were magic buttons that gave hot and cold water out of a spout. He had never seen anything like it. There weren't waste buckets either. Instead, Ildar had pointed out something he called a 'toilet', and once you did your business, another button magically whisked it away. No wonder the streets in Arcathia were so clean. Even though Havyn hadn't started his magic lessons with Ildar yet, he was enamoured of magic already. He hoped to learn some more of its secrets.

"He'll need some wizarding robes, too," said Severin to Iri, the royal tailor. "What do you think might suit?"

"With his colouring, purple would go well," replied Iri, a wizened old man with as many cracks in his face as old parchment. What little hair he had, just two tufts of it by his ears, was grey, as were his eyes. His back was stooped as if he spent a lot of time bent over sewing and cutting tables.

"No, not purple. My father would never allow that."

"Of course. How about a deep red? Or even jade? That would set off his dark hair brilliantly. How about some paler colours? Yellow or blue?" The tailor moved over to the bed where bolts of fabric in various hues lay. There were silks, linen, cotton, velvets, furs, and more, all haphazardly piled on Havyn's bed. Iri lifted up a swathe of pale yellow and draped it across Havyn's shoulders.

"No, not yellow," said Severin. "Try the jade and the ruby."

Once again, Havyn's shoulders were draped in the different fabrics. Iri and Severin both nodded. "Make a set in the jade and the ruby," said Severin. "He'll need new tunics and leggings as well as hose. And formal wear for the betrothal ceremony. I think the ruby would do for a formal robe."

"Of course, your highness. Anything else?"

"I think that's everything. Will you have it ready by the time we need to leave?"

"We'll get started right away. The wardrobe should be finished in about five days."

"Excellent. Thank you, Iri."

"What is going on in here?" demanded Ildar from the doorway. "Severin? What are you doing with my apprentice?"

"Iri and I were just sorting out Havyn's new wardrobe," said Severin, waving to Havyn that he could get dressed again. Havyn quickly pulled on the tunic and leggings Ildar had given him on his first night at the palace. A fierce blush heated his cheeks.

"Havyn is my apprentice!" snapped Ildar. "He is my responsibility. Furs and velvets? Silks? A wizard has no need for all of that. I will ensure Havyn gets all the clothing he needs, not you."

Havyn wondered how the wizard could talk back so forcefully to a prince without worrying about execution. Maybe wizards had no fear of death.

"He's my responsibility," protested Severin, his hands on his hips as he stared the wizard down. "I bought him. He's *mine!*"

Havyn's breath caught, and his heart beat frantically against his chest at the possessive way Severin had said it. None of his earlier Masters had ever spoken about him like that. Like they really wanted him.

Ildar's grey eyes narrowed. "Yours? Did you forget you signed his freedom papers, Severin? Havyn is not yours or any other man's. He is my apprentice because he wishes it, not because he is being given no other choice. Havyn is not a possession to be owned, I thought you realised that by now. Now leave us."

Severin looked like he was about to make some other retort, but he turned on his heel and stormed out, his boots clicking on the tiled floor. Iri hurried after him, carrying some of the fabrics with him, but most remained sitting on Havyn's bed. Havyn glanced at the fabrics, then at Ildar, feeling as if he had failed the wizard in some way.

Ildar seemed to sense it. "Havyn, I am not angry at you. It is very difficult to turn down the prince. I'm afraid he has been a little spoilt growing up so alone. It's not surprising, after his parents lost six brothers before him."

"Six?" Havyn gasped. "All his brothers died?"

"I'm afraid so, but Severin doesn't know he ever had any brothers. They all died in infancy. When Severin was born, his mother was very ill, too. Severin has never been blessed with perfect health, and there were times during his childhood when the king and queen thought they would lose him, too. No wonder he is spoilt. I will have more words to say to him about this, but please don't feel upset. I should have organised some fittings for you sooner. I have other duties around the palace, but that shouldn't mean that I neglect the needs of my apprentice. Severin is right that you do need some more clothes, but he should have left it up to me."

"I'm all right," said Havyn. "You don't need to worry about me."

"Can you read and write, Havyn?"

"Yes, sir. I did the accounting books for my last Master. I acted as his clerk for reading and writing letters. He didn't know his letters."

"Indeed, it seems it's becoming more common for the nobility to let their children run riot, not even learning the basics anymore.

Fortunately, that was not the case with Prince Severin. I was his tutor for many years. He knows his letters and his accounting. I made sure of it. Very well, come with me," said Ildar, placing a hand in the small of Havyn's back and ushering him out of his bedroom and down a dark corridor.

Havyn paused, seeing something shimmering on the wall at the end of the corridor. "There's something there," Havyn said, glancing back over his shoulder at Ildar.

"Yes, there is a ward there, you can sense it? What does it feel like?"

"I'm not sure. It's like I can see something...sparkly? Silver and gold," said Havyn. "Like little stars."

"Close your eyes and move toward the wall," suggested Ildar.

Havyn did so. He felt the silver and gold stars of the ward pass over his body. Even before he opened his eyes, Havyn knew he wasn't going to see the corridor anymore. The air in this room felt different. He could feel sunlight on his face, although there were no windows in the corridor.

"You can open them now," said Ildar, chuckling.

Havyn did so and found himself in a bookcase-lined room. The books were piled so high up toward the ceiling that there were ladders leaning against a few of them in order to reach. Three walls were taken up with the books, the other held floor-length windows whose stained glass were casting multi-coloured shadows on the wooden floor.

There were three desks in the room. Two were covered in scrolls, parchments, quills, and inkwells, while the third held a row of leather-bound books and a map. There were couches and soft chairs dotted about the room, as if inviting people to sink into them and read for a while.

"Welcome to my library, Havyn," said Ildar. "Of course, I say my library, when, in fact, it is the royal wizarding library. Only wizards can access this room since it is so well warded. Soon you will be the next royal wizard, so it will become your library."

"What?" asked Havyn, gaping at the wizard.

"You are my apprentice, Havyn. That means that I am training you to replace me. I'm not going to live forever, no matter what strange tales you may have heard about wizards. We are mortal, just like anyone else."

"But I don't want you to die!" Havyn stared at him wide-eyed.

"Well, I have no intention of dropping dead tomorrow. I hope to have quite a few more years in me yet. It usually takes five years to train an apprentice, so you'll have plenty of time to get used to the idea."

Havyn didn't want to get used to the idea. The thought that Ildar might die soon was something he preferred not to dwell on, so he just nodded.

"Now, you said you can read and write?"

"Yes, sir."

"Very well, I'd like you to read this book and then write me a chapter summary to show that you've understood it. I will be attending to my court duties this afternoon. This evening we can go over what you've done. We can discuss anything you don't understand later."

Ildar waved his hand at a bookshelf, and a black leather-bound book smacked into his hand. Havyn gaped, and Ildar laughed at him. "We'll soon have you doing that, too, Havyn. Don't worry. Now there are quills and ink on the desks there. In the desk drawer is a knife in case you need to sharpen your quill. I think there should be enough ink. If you run out, there is a storage cupboard in the next room." Ildar waved to a wooden doorway that Havyn hadn't seen when they'd first entered the library. "I'll leave the wards up, so you shouldn't be disturbed. They are attuned to you now. If you need to leave, just do what you did before. I'd suggest keeping your eyes closed again. Trying to walk through walls can be a bit disconcerting at first."

Havyn glanced down at the title embossed in gold foil on the leather. *An Apprentice's Guide to the Magical Arts and Sciences.* It was a slim volume. Havyn didn't think it would take him that long to read, but writing the chapter summaries might take some time. He'd probably be doing it for the rest of the day.

"I'll have lunch sent to you shortly," said Ildar. "So don't be too worried when it appears out of nowhere."

"Thank you," said Havyn. Ildar bade him good day. Once he was gone, Havyn made his way over to one of the couches in order to start reading. He'd read the book thoroughly first, then do it chapter by chapter before writing his summaries.

The lunch appeared just like Ildar had said it would. Havyn traced the map of Arcathia with his fingers while he ate his bread and cheese. He washed it down with a mug of ale that made his head ache a little. Havyn was used to drinking little else but water, and sometimes, he'd never even gotten that.

It was dark by the time Ildar returned to the library. The lanterns on the walls had come to life automatically when the sun had set, so

Havyn was still bent over his work. He'd filled rolls of parchment already. His hand was sore from so much writing, and quite often, he'd had to rest to ease the cramps. His thumb and forefinger were smudged with blue ink, and he looked up at Ildar in some alarm.

"I have just three more chapters to do, but I can get them done soon, I promise!" he gabbled.

"Havyn, lad. Calm down. I only meant for you to do the first chapter. Are you telling me you've read the whole book and attempted to summarise each chapter?"

"Yes, sir. Wasn't that what you wanted?"

"You must be a very fast reader, but did you understand what you read? Can you tell me the First Law of Magic?"

"Magic is not a replacement for nature. All magic has to balance or there will be chaos in the world."

"Indeed. Well, Havyn. It looks like you might become a master wizard in less than five years after all."

Chapter Seven

Severin dropped his sword. A sharp pain had shot up his arm when Kelandra unarmed him with a flick of her own weapon. Kelandra flung a braid over her shoulder, sheathed her sword, and shook her head. "That was terrible, even for you," she said. "Didn't you practice at all while you were away?" It was a fortnight since they'd returned to the castle, but it was the first time Severin had taken up his practice sword again

All around them, other warriors practiced, too. Some engaged in fencing like he and Kelandra attempted, others fought with javelins or spears. Some wrestled bare handed or attacked each other with quarterstaffs. Further away, the archers fired practice arrows at makeshift targets of hay and straw. Severin couldn't see them, but he knew that in the tiltyards on the other side of the palace the cavalry practiced their jousting skills. They always had to be prepared for war.

"I'm fine, thanks for asking," said Severin sarcastically, shaking his hand and trying to avoid looking at one particular corner of the courtyard where Havyn sat with a book on his lap listening intently to whatever Ildar had to say. Apparently, the wizard was teaching him something if the way he was waving his hands about was any indication. It reminded Severin of his own days of being tutored. Severin felt a pang beneath his breastbone, not sure why he was feeling so sad about Ildar teaching Havyn. He flushed with shame when he remembered what he'd said to the wizard—that Havyn was his because he'd bought him. Was Severin becoming like the Oscians already? Unable to see each man for his own person but something to be owned—enslaved?

"Oh, stop whining, Severin. I know you're fine. What's the matter with you lately? You've been so miserable since you got back. Not that you were a joy to behold before you left, mind you. Anyone would think you had never even had your initiation yet. What's gotten into you?" asked Kelandra

"Nothing. I'm just distracted," said Severin, his eyes flickered to the corner where Ildar was deep in discussion with his apprentice.

Havyn was dressed in one of the jade green robes Severin had asked Iri for. Severin had to agree with the tailor, the colour set off Havyn's complexion perfectly. Severin sighed and sheathed his sword. He was done for the day, no matter how much his father wanted him to be a warrior.

Kelandra glanced behind her then back at Severin, a knowing glint in her green eyes. "Oh. I see. He is quite handsome, I suppose, but what would I know? I'm married to my sword." Kelandra chuckled.

"Do you ever regret your vows, Kelandra? That you gave up marriage and family in order to protect me?"

"It's how the Daughters of the Sword have always been, Severin. If I wanted to get married I would have to leave. My vows aren't permanent and it's an honour to be chosen. I've always wanted to become a Daughter. It's much easier to stay focused if we aren't concentrating on romance. I've never really missed it."

"Romance. Is that what this is? I don't know what to do," said Severin, wiping the sweat from his brow. Kelandra had barely worked up a sweat, yet here Severin was panting like a fox being chased by the hounds. "I never went through with the initiation. I'm not considered a man until I'm no longer a virgin. But how could I go through with it? I'm not interested in women. Now I can't stop thinking about him!"

Not to mention the dreams. Every morning Severin woke up with sticky sheets and groin. He was sure the laundry maids were gossiping about it behind his back, but no one had ever said anything to his face. Maybe Ildar was right. A demon was after his soul. A demon with dark hair and violet eyes named Havyn.

"Have you told him?" Kelandra asked, as if it would be that easy.

"Told him what? I'm getting betrothed to Ythrin in less than a week. Ildar will never allow Havyn anywhere near me, not if he knows how I feel. You know Ildar's thoughts on sex and magic—the two shouldn't mix."

"So you're just lusting after Havyn? If that's all it is, why don't you go to the city and find someone there to bed? I'm sure there'd be plenty of lads lining up to bed the prince."

Severin had not thought about seeking out a replacement for the object of his desire. "That's not what I want," Severin said. "I don't want anyone else. I've never felt like this before. I only want Havyn."

Kelandra smiled and caressed his cheek, a sisterly gesture that had never made Severin's heart race. Not like when he caught unexpected glimpses of Havyn throughout the palace. It was as if Havyn was a flame that Severin was drawn to like a moth, and he didn't care if that flame consumed him.

"Well then, Severin. I don't think you're in lust at all. You're in love."

"But how do I know?"

"Maybe you should go to the temple and consult the Oracle. You might get some answers."

"Answers? Aye, cryptic ones maybe. You know I don't hold with all that prophecy stuff. I haven't been to the temple for years."

"I know. Maybe that's why you're so restless? You need a higher power to guide you sometimes, Severin. We all do."

"All right. All right. I'll try it. It can't hurt, can it?"

* * * *

The temple sat just outside the palace precincts, a white rectangular building with fluted columns and carvings of ravens all along them. When Severin entered the coolness of the colonnade, it was like entering a different world. He could no longer hear the noise from the streets outside, although he could still see Arcathians going about their daily business at the nearby markets.

Severin jumped. He hadn't heard the priestess approach, so when he looked up, surprise filled him upon his discovery that she was directly in front of him. Like all Priestesses of the Raven, the woman had long black hair that flowed unbound to her waist. A white mask hid her face, and beneath her white silk gown, her feet were bare with the nails painted jet black. She didn't speak. All the Priestesses took a vow of silence, broken only when the Raven Mother spoke through them.

"I wish to seek an audience with Raven Mother's Oracle," said Severin, crossing his arms over his chest and bowing respectfully.

The priestess pointed to his boots. Severin bent down and tugged them off, setting them on the shelf that jutted out at waist height from the wall of the colonnade. Once that was done, the priestess beckoned him forward. Severin followed her through a wooden doorway to the inner sanctum of the temple. There were four altars in the sanctum, one for each of the four winds—North, South, East, and West. By the base of the North altar shone a blue lantern, red for South, purple for West, and orange for East.

In the centre of the room, the Oracle sat cross-legged on the floor draped in heavy shawls, her head shaved bald. The woman was a lot younger than Severin had expected, and beneath the shawls, was the swell of a pregnant belly. He'd always imagined the Oracle to be some gap-toothed crone, not a pregnant woman about his own age. A fire pit blazed in front of the Oracle. The smoke and heat burned Severin's lungs so badly his lungs ached and his eyes stung.

"Who approaches the Great Mother?" asked the Oracle, her eyes stared at a point somewhere beyond Severin. She was blind, as all the Arcathian Oracles had been.

"Severin," he replied, knowing that his rank meant nothing here. Severin knew that as far as the goddess and her Oracle were concerned, Severin was just like any other man.

"Be welcome, Severin. Sit." The Oracle waved at the floor on the other side of the fire pit. The priestess bowed and left them alone. "What have you brought for your sacrifice?"

Severin removed a small dagger from his belt. "Is my blood acceptable to Raven Mother?"

"It is. Just a drop. Our Mother is not greedy."

Severin nodded then realised she couldn't see him do it. He sliced his palm open and allowed two drops of his blood to fall into the fire, both of them hissing as they did so.

"Two. Most generous. The Raven Mother will be pleased. Stare into the fire, Severin. Perhaps you will see the answers you seek."

"Thank you, Gracious One."

Severin stared at the flickering flames, wondering what answers he was, in fact, looking for. His mind wandered to Havyn, to Ythrin, the unknown princess, to his parents, to Ildar, and to Severin's own lack of magical abilities. Both his parents had been good at magic, but it seemed their talent had not been passed down to their son. For a while, Severin could see nothing other than the flames, but then they wavered in front of his eyes and he saw random fragments.

Severin saw his mother sobbing over a dead infant, Ildar at the prow of a boat, holding his wizard staff aloft at a storm-tossed sea with Havyn by his side. He saw the White Palace of Ravensfell in ruins—two armies marching against each other, one bearing aloft the device of the Brotherhood of the Raven the other the device of the Daughters of the Sword. The royal guards fighting each other? The blue and orange of the fire wavered again and he saw himself holding a baby with a thatch of raven hair, smiling down at it.

"What did you see?" asked the Oracle.

"Dreams. The future? I don't know."

"It is only a possible path. Nothing is set in stone. We make our own way, Severin. You have to decide which journey you wish to take. We always have a choice, but our decisions affect the future. Has it helped you decide, young Severin?"

Severin wondered how she knew he was young.

"I think so. Thank you, Gracious One."

Severin knew now what he must do. He remembered seeing the guards fighting each other. Hadn't his father warned him there would be civil war if Severin didn't produce an heir? That's what he reckoned the vision was telling him. But what about his mother and the dead child? That didn't make much sense, nor did Ildar and Havyn on the prow of a boat trying to calm a storm. The baby at the end was his and Princess Ythrin's heir, the solution to the trouble between Arcathia and Oscia. No matter how much he might want Havyn, Severin couldn't sacrifice his people's happiness for his own. He had to marry Princess Ythrin, and try to forget about Havyn.

Easier said than done. Ildar was training Havyn to take his place as the next royal wizard and advisor. Of course, he could always ask Ildar to seek out another apprentice, but Severin knew that wouldn't go down well with Ildar. For years, Ildar had searched for someone equal to his powers, to no avail. Now that he had found the one he favoured, Severin knew Ildar wouldn't let his apprentice go just because Severin was attracted to him. Havyn had no doubt already heard Ildar's views on sex—that a wizard should remain celibate in order to fully appreciate their powers, so it was probably a moot point anyway. Havyn wouldn't want to be his lover, but Severin spent a few minutes daydreaming about making Havyn his royal consort, a male lover with all the privileges of a royal wife, but none of the responsibilities. No one expected a male consort to produce an heir.

Severin stood and found the priestess by his side again, as if she'd appeared from nowhere. "Thank you." He crossed his arms over his chest and bowed first to the Oracle, then again to the priestess before taking his leave and retrieving his shoes.

When Severin left the temple, his heart was lighter than it had been in a while. He knew now what he was supposed to do. Perhaps Kelandra had been right and he'd just needed a prod in the right direction.

* * * *

The priestess sank down in front of the Oracle and caressed the swell of the other woman's belly.

"He didn't understand the visions," the Oracle said. "But he will. He will."

Chapter Eight

Havyn stretched and yawned when he awoke to the sunlight flooding his bedchamber. The warmth was a gentle reminder that it was time to get up and not linger. When he'd been a slave, more often than not, he'd just been kicked awake by his Master or Mistress and made to work straightaway, sometimes without time for breakfast. Here, Ildar didn't seem to have a set timetable for Havyn's studies. It was whenever Ildar had the time from his other duties. When Ildar wasn't around to supervise him, he left work for Havyn, but expected Havyn to have time to himself too.

Despite the warmth through the windows, the tiled floor was always cold, so Havyn climbed down from his bed and slid his feet into the slippers Ildar had given him before heading to the bathroom for his morning ablutions. Havyn smiled to himself while he made his way to the bath to turn on the water. While waiting for the bath to fill, he used the toilet and washed his hands. There were shelves filled with bottles of fragrant oils that Ildar had brewed himself, not to mention all the different soaps and shampoos. Looking at his face in the mirror above the basin, Havyn checked to see if he had started growing any hair there yet. One of the maids always left out razors and shaving brushes for him, but so far Havyn never had need of them. He had no body hair at all, and sometimes, the other slaves had teased him about it. Havyn wondered if it was because he'd been starved so often that his development seemed to be so slow.

He took a quick bath and got dressed in his jade green robes with an under tunic and leggings in a paler green. Ildar had postponed lessons for the day. The whole Court was making its way to Oscia for Severin's betrothal ceremony. Havyn would travel as Ildar's apprentice. Severin's presence had dwindled to almost nothing since the fuss over Havyn's wardrobe. Afforded only the occasional glimpse in the corridors, or when he was out in the practice yards, Havyn couldn't get Severin out of his head. Oh, how he wished the prince wasn't getting married. However, Havyn knew that choice wasn't up to him. He understood why a prince needed to marry and beget an heir, but it still hurt to think of Severin with another. Havyn didn't know how he was going to bear it.

Ildar informed him that once Severin married the princess, the prince would live in Oscia...so would Ildar and Havyn, as his advisors. Could Havyn cope with seeing the prince making eyes at his new bride every day? Havyn knew it was never going to be for him. He was a wizard, and Ildar had made it quite clear he expected Havyn to remain celibate. That was how a wizard kept his power. Havyn often wondered if such a sacrifice was worth it, even for magic.

* * * *

Queen Yinare wasn't well enough to travel, but most of the rest of the Court was there, including Lady Kessarie, the queen's chief lady-in-waiting. Kelandra rolled her eyes when the courtier wasn't looking, and Havyn tried not to laugh. Kessarie looked put out when she saw Kelandra sitting on her horse next to the prince. Kelandra would ride as Prince Severin's main escort, she was his chief guard, but it was clear to Havyn that Kessarie wished it was her who would ride next to the prince.

Havyn had never ridden a horse, so he and Ildar were in one of the carriages toward the back of the column with the other non-riders. King Faran was dressed in a purple cloak with a gold circlet adorning his head, but little other jewellery. Bandits preyed on travellers on the wooded roads between Arcathia and Oscia. Advertising one's wealth in such a way would not be wise.

Havyn wondered if any of the bandits would be fooled because all of the bodyguards were dressed in their royal devices—the raven tunics for the king's bodyguard and the golden sword for the prince's. Maybe it would have been better if they'd just travelled as they had before, with Severin and Ildar dressed like travellers rather than all this fanfare.

Trumpeters on the ramparts blew their instruments, and soon, the whole party moved out, the crowds cheering and waving them on their way. The city's inhabitants threw flowers on the road as they made their way down the avenue and out of the city gates. It was quite exciting to be part of it. For a short time, Havyn forgot that all of this was because of Severin's upcoming marriage.

It took a while for them to get out of the city because so many well-wishers stopped Severin to ply him with good luck kisses and presents, which one of the servants put into a luggage cart. The rocking of the carriage along the cobbled streets made Havyn feel ill. He was glad that their coach wasn't enclosed with glass like some of the others. There was a shade they could pull up if the sun got too hot, or if it rained, but as yet, they hadn't needed to use it.

Havyn looked around at everything going on outside, trying to distract himself from the swaying. He didn't want to throw up in front of all these people. Severin was accepting all the kisses and presents bestowed upon him with good grace, or at least he seemed to be. Havyn could sense the reality, Severin just wanted to get to Oscia and get the wedding over and done with.

When the carriage jolted over a rather large rut in the road, Havyn groaned, holding onto the side of the carriage, his stomach roiling. Beside him, Ildar rummaged in one of the many pockets of his robes and lifted out a silver flask. "Here, Havyn. Drink this."

"What is it?"

"Ginger tea. It will help with the nausea."

"Thank you." Havyn took a few sips of the liquid. The tea was cold, but it had a fire all its own. He sputtered a little, then handed it back to the wizard. Indeed, he felt much better, and even managed a small smile for Ildar.

"Will it take as long to get back to Oscia?"

"No, we're going to the capital, which is just over the Arcathian border. With the horses and wagons, it'll take less time than when we had to walk. The countries were, in fact, one kingdom many years ago, but there was a falling out between twin brothers over who should inherit the throne, and so they split the kingdom in two."

"So both royal families are related?"

"Distantly, the split happened such a long time ago. It's nothing that would prevent marriage between the two families now."

"Oh," Havyn said. No chance of the marriage being called off because of that then. "I've never been to a wedding."

"Well, the only one I've been to was King Faran's and Queen Yinare's years ago," said Ildar. "Things are probably done a lot differently in Oscia."

"Maybe not. Perhaps they kept the same traditions as in Arcathia."

"Perhaps," said Ildar.

"So that's why I could understand you," said Havyn, just now realising that he had been talking with the Arcathians in the same language he'd used all his life. "We speak Arcathian in Oscia?"

"Well done, my lad. I never noticed that, Havyn. Yes, our language is the same, but I will be teaching you some of the other common languages as part of your studies. You'll need to know them to help Severin deal with foreign dignitaries. Languages were not his strong suit."

Havyn let Ildar ramble on about Severin's childhood tutoring, keen to find out as much about the prince as possible without actually asking anyone about him. He wanted to know, but didn't want everyone else to know how interested he was in the prince. Although now that he was being trained as Ildar's replacement, perhaps it wouldn't seem that out of place to ask.

They eventually left the city and made their way along the country tracks between the woods. Both countries were heavily wooded outside of the cities with most farming communities a lot further inland. Havyn had never seen a farm, although he'd gone to the markets for his Masters in order to acquire food and textiles from the farmers trading there. It was the only time Havyn had been given money. Woe betide him if his Master thought he'd paid too much for the goods! He received a clip round the ear if he was lucky and a whipping if he wasn't. Havyn closed his eyes, shivering in remembrance, almost as if he could feel the whip falling down on his back again.

The party stopped for lunch in a wooded glade. Havyn was surprised to find the courtiers lifted out a table with separate legs, which they attached, along with dining chairs, napery, plates, and silverware. As a royal advisor, Ildar ate at the table along with Severin and his father, but since, for the moment, Havyn was just an apprentice, he ate with the other skilled apprentices, who found fallen logs to sit on and eat their meal.

Havyn had never spent much time with them. They were all studying to be carpenters, smiths, chandlers, fletchers, and other tradesmen. Despite not having anything in common with Havyn, they welcomed him warmly into their little group and shared the food and drink. No one mentioned his origins. Havyn sometimes wondered if everyone knew he had been a slave, or if Severin and Ildar had kept it secret. It was going to be difficult going back to Oscia. What if the Oscians didn't accept Severin's freedom papers? What if he was captured and sold yet again? Havyn shuddered when a cloud passed over the sun. A couple of the other apprentices made a sign to ward off evil.

"That's a bad omen, that is," said one of them, a boy of around ten or eleven. "It means bad luck's coming."

"That's just country superstition," said another, older apprentice. He mock wrestled the younger one to the ground. "Anyone would think you'd come straight in off the fields!"

"I was born in the city," the boy retorted indignantly while the two of them fought some more. After a while, they both had to stop because they were giggling so much. Havyn smiled at them, glad the apprentices got on with one another. Sometimes in the households he'd served, the slaves had a distinct hierarchy, and it was as common to receive punishment from another slave as it was from the Master.

Once the king and his entourage had finished their meal, it was time for everyone else to complete theirs. The tables and trappings were packed up and everyone made their way back to their horses or their coaches. When Havyn sat down in the carriage next to Ildar, the wizard offered him another sip of the ginger tea. Havyn took it gratefully.

It was almost dark when someone near King Faran screamed loudly. Havyn and Ildar leant out at each side of the carriage to see what was going on. Almost in slow motion, Havyn watched Severin catch his father as he fell, a black feathered arrow sticking out from Faran's shoulder. He'd been shot. There was very little blood, but Havyn could see how pale the king's face had become. His lips were already turning blue.

"Look to the king! Look to the king!" screamed Kelandra, her sword in the air as she rallied her troops. The Brotherhood of the Raven galloped toward Severin. Chayal removed the king's body from Severin's arms and tumbled Severin to the ground. More arrows whistled through the air to the screams and cries of the women and children. Some of the guards made their way into the woods to try to find the culprits, others helped people down from the horses and buggies, making them all lie on the ground while arrows continued to rain down on them.

Havyn climbed down from the carriage and made his way to Faran's still body. The nearer he got to the king, the worse he felt. There was something wrong with the arrow, something *other*. Something supernatural. It wasn't an ordinary arrow. It was like looking at despair. Havyn reached out to touch it, but recoiled in horror at the depth of hate coming from it. He sensed treachery and deception. He reached out to try and touch it again, but he was pulled down next to Severin.

"Don't! The Oscians dip their arrows in poison," growled Chayal as Havyn fell heavily on both of them.

Some of the returning guards shook their heads. Havyn stood to allow the other men to get up.

Severin looked like he might be sick. His gaze never left his father's body. Chayal knelt, followed by the Raven Brotherhood and the Daughters of the Sword.

"The King is dead. Long live the King! Long Live the King! All Hail King Severin! All Hail King Severin!"

Chapter Nine

The words reached Severin through a dark haze. "All Hail King Severin! All Hail King Severin!" Among the chants of the brotherhood, more screams came from some of the women and the younger apprentices. Severin looked from his father's unmoving body to Havyn kneeling by his father's shoulder.

"Heal him!" Severin roared so loudly that Havyn jumped, looking enquiringly.

"Sire?" asked Havyn, his voice shaking.

"You're a wizard, aren't you? Heal him! I command that you heal him."

"Master Severin, he's gone. He can't be healed," said Havyn. "I'm sorry. Your father is dead." Havyn stood, dusted his robes free of grass, loose leaves, and dirt. Dirt that even now Faran was lying in. He'd be filthy soon.

"How dare you spew such lies!" ranted Severin. Faran couldn't be dead. The man was as unmovable as a mountain and about as unchanging. His father couldn't be dead. This was a trick. It had to be. Havyn looked at him, and then at the guards like he expected them to agree with him. "He's just wounded! He isn't dead! He isn't dead!"

"Severin, the lad's right," said Chayal, taking a firm hold of Severin's arm, trying to take him away from his father and from Havyn. Severin fought with all his strength to remove himself from the bodyguard's hold. Severin wrenched free and bore down on Havyn like an avenging angel.

"Don't lie to me! Don't ever lie to me!" shrieked Severin. He punched Havyn in the face. There was a crunch of bone, and the force of his blow made Havyn stagger backward holding his jaw. Blood dripped from Havyn's nose while he stared hard at Severin, eyes welling up with unshed tears.

"I've never lied to you. Never," said Havyn, turning and fleeing somewhere beyond Severin's reach. His hand stung where he'd hit the young wizard, and Severin stared hard at it, as though it were not his own. There was a hollow ache beneath his breastbone. Severin had no idea what had just come over him.

"Severin!" roared Ildar, his robes billowing behind him as he cut a swathe through the guards and the courtiers. "How dare you assault my apprentice? I don't care if you are the king. You're still young enough to bend over my knee! Your father is dead, Severin. Hitting Havyn is not going to bring him back."

"No, he's just wounded. Look," said Severin, bending down and listening to his father's chest. "His heart's still beating. I can hear it."

"No, lad," said Ildar, kneeling down and wrapping his arms around him, tugging him away from his father. "It's your own heart you can hear. Not your father's. Come away, Severin. Let the warriors prepare his final resting place."

"No! He can't leave me. He never told me! He never told me!" Severin sobbed, not caring how many people were watching. Ildar rocked him. The man whispered soothing words that Severin had always wanted to hear from his father. Severin could hardly remember a time when his father had addressed him with little other than scorn and loathing, but he had seemed to warm to Severin now that he'd agreed to marriage. It was such a waste. Severin would never gain his approval. Never. It was the only thing he'd ever wanted, and the one thing that had been constantly out of his reach. Not once had his father ever told him he loved him, and now he never would.

Ildar began singing to him, a lullaby from Severin's childhood. Severin turned and muffled his sobs against Ildar's shoulder. Severin's whole body trembled with the force of his weeping. Ildar rubbed his back and continued to sing to him, helping to soothe his aching heart. It reminded Severin of all the times when he'd been ill as a child and Ildar had been the one to tend him. It was Ildar who had read him bedtime tales and played with him. Faran had never been interested in anything except how suitable a warrior his son might become. Ildar may have threatened to put Severin over his knee, but in truth Ildar had never punished him physically. It was Faran's hands that had brought him pain, never Ildar's. Severin knew Ildar wasn't an easy man to love. He was bossy and overbearing most of the time, but Severin loved him for he was the nearest thing to a real father Severin had ever had.

Severin didn't know how long he lay there accepting the comfort of Ildar's embrace while the darkness crept upon them like a thief. Torches and fires were soon lit all around him. People milled around, whispering about him, no doubt wondering if he would go mad like King Eltan had.

King. He was now the King of Arcathia. Severin struggled out of Ildar's embrace and ran to the edge of the woods. He sank to his knees, retching until it felt like he had torn his innards out through his mouth.

A few moments later, Ildar was next to him, offering him a goblet of water. Severin drank the water, and then threw the goblet in the undergrowth. "This is what got him killed! Riding to Oscia with the full Court, with all his gold and finery. Begone, all of you. Get back to the palace where you belong!"

"Sire, the Raven Brotherhood's duty is to guard the king," said Chayal, not making any attempt to leave.

"And what about us? Are you going to take over as Severin's guard when the Daughters of the Sword have been guarding him since he was born?" demanded Kelandra. "Severin is our responsibility."

"When he was a prince, yes. Now he is the king, he is our responsibility."

"Stop it! My father is dead and all you two can do is bicker? Ildar, can you arrange a burial for my father when you get back to the palace?"

"I am not going back to the palace," said Ildar, resting his hand on his staff. "Havyn and I are going with you to see King Eltan. You need Havyn's skills. No arguments."

Severin nodded, feeling too drained to try and argue with the wizard. Once Ildar made up his mind, it stayed made up.

"Chayal?"

"I'm not leaving either, Sire. It would be remiss of me to allow you to travel through Oscia unguarded, especially now. No one else was hurt. This was an assassination."

Severin turned to Kelandra, he knew even before asking that she was not turning back either. The Daughters had always taken their role as his protectors seriously. Severin knew Kelandra was not going to allow him to sneak off without her ever again. Well, Chayal and Kelandra could stay then, but he wasn't having the rest of them follow him all over Oscia.

"Is there someone here who can take my father's body back for burial?" Severin screamed into the night. No one moved, probably unsure if they would receive the same treatment Havyn had.

"I'll arrange it with one of my men, Sire," said Chayal. "But your father was a Raven Warrior. We don't bury warriors."

"You don't? What do you do with your dead?"

"Do you know the Raven Tower?"

"I've heard of it, but my mother forbids me to go there."

"It's where all warriors are left. It can be upsetting if you don't know our customs."

"Left? What do you mean 'left'?" demanded Severin.

"There are ledges fitted around each floor of the tower by every window. Warriors are left there for Raven Mother."

"What? You mean to leave him out like carrion?" Severin stared at them, horrified tears burning the back of his throat. There was no way he was going to allow that to happen to his father. "No! I forbid it. He will be buried. I insist upon it."

"Sire, that is not what your father would have wanted. There is no honour if he denies the Raven Mother."

"My father is dead and I want him buried!" screamed Severin. "Or do you disobey your king, Chayal?"

Chayal shook his head. "It will be as you command." Chayal turned and sought out one of the other guards. When he found him, they argued frantically. No doubt about Severin's request for a burial rather than to leave his father at the Tower.

"Ildar, I want them all gone," said Severin, waving at the courtiers and apprentices still milling around. "Send them back to Arcathia. We'll make the rest of the journey incognito like we did before. I don't want all these people around me. It's too much."

"Of course, Severin. I will send them on their way."

"Severin, you can't mean for me to leave," said Lady Kessarie as she approached the small group. "I'm your mother's representative to Oscia. I have to go with you!"

"No, you don't. You need to go back home and tell my mother what's happened."

Kessarie pouted, but Severin would not be swayed. He was under no delusions, he knew Kessarie desired him. The fact that she'd turned up at his initiation hadn't surprised him in the least. When Severin had picked none of the ladies, Kessarie had been the only one who had seemed overly disappointed. Even if Severin had desired women, Kessarie wouldn't have interested him. He didn't think she was interested in him either, she probably hoped for advancement. Severin suspected she would be quite happy to have become Queen of Arcathia after his mother. He wondered if his mother's illness had been entirely natural after all.

"Go home, Kessarie, and if I hear another word of complaint, I'll have you arrested."

"What? I haven't done anything!"

"No? Doesn't it seem strange that my mother, who was in perfect health recently, suddenly became ill when we needed to travel to Oscia for my betrothal?"

Kessarie flushed. "You don't know what you're talking about. I had nothing to do with it." She glared at him.

"Go home. That is an order from your king," said Severin coldly. "Or shall we add traitor to the charges?"

"How dare you accuse me of such vileness!" Kessarie yelled at him. She stalked off and climbed into one the carriages with some of the other ladies-in-waiting.

Severin was glad to see her go.

* * * *

Two hours later, Severin stared morosely into the campfire with his four companions sitting silently around him. Havyn was as far away from him as possible, but maybe that was for the best. The rest of the Court was now on their way back to Arcathia with his father's body. Oh, Raven, what were they going to tell his mother?

"Why did the Oscians murder my father?" Severin asked so softly that he wasn't sure whether or not the others heard him or if he even wanted them to. There was only one reason Severin continued on his journey to King Eltan's palace, and that was to avenge his father. If Eltan thought for one minute that Severin would marry his niece after this, he was very wrong.

"He wasn't murdered by Oscians," said Ildar gravely.

"What? It was their arrow," Severin growled, clenching his fist.

"Havyn, come here," said Ildar, beckoning to his apprentice. Havyn's eyes reflected the firelight, and it was like his eyes glowed in the dark. Severin's heart lurched so far up in his chest it was a wonder it didn't fly out from his throat. He couldn't cope with Havyn. Not now. Not after everything. "The arrows weren't Oscian, but disguised to look like them. Someone wants us to think the Oscians were to blame. Havyn had sensed the deception straightaway. Isn't that right, Havyn?"

"Yes, sir," Havyn said, not meeting Severin's eyes. His face was starting to look a bit bruised around the eyes, and seeing the physical reminder of Severin's violence made his heart ache.

"Who would do that, and then blame the Oscians?"

"I don't know, Severin, but perhaps we will discover the truth if we make our way to Oscia as planned."

"And risk another ambush?"

"It should be less likely now. Someone was after the king, and knew who he was. Perhaps the assassin hoped to stop the marriage and plunge both countries into war again. Wars have been fought between our nations for lesser things. Maybe they don't yet know what you look like. Travelling like this will be less obvious."

"Were you always this sensible, Ildar?" asked Severin, glad that someone seemed to be thinking straight. Not an Oscian ambush, but who? Severin didn't doubt Havyn, the youth was a Truth Seeker—a rare breed of wizard who could sense lies and deception as easily as if the culprits had told him their secrets himself. He wondered if Havyn could sense how Severin felt about him. He resolved to keep his mind as shuttered as possible. Not that he was sure how Havyn's gift worked. Havyn said he could sense things, but Severin wouldn't put it past him to be able to read minds like a book.

Chapter Ten

Near the campfire, Havyn sat close to Ildar. Staring into the flames helped to soothe him. Sometimes, if he stared long enough, he could almost see pictures flickering there. He loved the crackling sound the wood made while it burned. Havyn was conscious of Severin's eyes on him, but Severin was quick to look away when Havyn saw him. Every time the prince—no, the king—watched him, Havyn had to rub his cheekbone. It still stung, but he wasn't sure whether the pain was real or just an echo of the pain he'd endured before. Whenever Havyn had been whipped or beaten, when he remembered the pain, it was as if he was feeling it again, so he was always in pain longer than any of the other slaves.

"You should get some sleep," said Kelandra from Havyn's other side. "Chayal and I will take turns at watch." Both Chayal and Kelandra were sharpening their swords with whetstones by the light of the fire, and the noise made Havyn shiver. He would rather have kept moving, but he knew how much Ildar hated travelling in the dark. Creatures rustled in the undergrowth around them, and Havyn wondered if any of them were as dangerous as the people with the arrows. There might be wolves or worse in the forest.

"Here," said Severin, tossing a blanket out of his pack. It landed in the dirt by Havyn's feet. Was that supposed to be some sort of apology? If Severin thought it was going to be that easy, he was wrong. Havyn didn't pick up the blanket. He glowered at Severin, then stomped further into the trees, and as far away from Severin as he could get without putting himself or the others in danger. Havyn could still see the fire and the shadows of his companions around it from where he stood. Even before he removed his robe to use as a pillow, he knew it was going to be a long night.

* * * *

Havyn jerked awake, panting harshly as the scenes from the nightmare lingered in the darkness. In the dream, Severin had Havyn manacled to a dungeon wall and carved words into his chest with a rusty knife. Over and over again, the word *mine* had been etched into his flesh, his blood dripping crimson onto the stone floor beneath his feet. Havyn frantically pulled the laces of his tunic apart and stared at his chest, but apart from his previous scars, it was unmarked. He heaved a sigh of relief.

When Havyn glanced toward the fire, he saw three shadows lying down and one sitting up. Knowing he wasn't going to get back to sleep, he made his way to the campfire and sat down beside Kelandra. He hugged his knees to his chest.

"Couldn't sleep?" asked Kelandra softly.

"Nightmare," said Havyn, staring at his knees while he spoke. He lifted his head. It had been a while since he'd had nightmares, and he knew it was because of Severin's behaviour that evening. Still, he couldn't quite believe that Severin had hit him. "He hates me now, doesn't he?"

"Oh, Havyn. I don't think that's the problem at all. Grief does strange things to people. Severin loved his father. He wanted only to please him, but his father was never satisfied with anything Severin did. Now that he's dead, Severin knows he will never get his father's approval. I don't think Severin meant to hurt you, Havyn. In fact, I've never seen him that violent before. He doesn't even like our practices at arms. Severin only did them to gain his father's approval, but he hated it. He would much rather read a book."

"That doesn't excuse what he did," said Havyn. "He shouldn't have hit me."

"No, he shouldn't have," agreed Kelandra. "He regrets it, and I'm sure he'd apologise if you'd let him."

Havyn knew he would probably accept the apology. He liked Severin, but he'd been severely disappointed in his behaviour. Havyn thought Severin above such things, but he knew deep in his heart Severin hadn't meant to hurt him. His senses were well aware of that fact—it was difficult to hide true emotions from a Seeker.

"Oh. Is it true warriors are left out for the crows?" Havyn wanted to talk and keep the silence of the night at bay.

"Well, it's what the Brotherhood of the Raven do. It's their custom. We're warriors, but our custom is different."

"What's your custom?"

"We bury our dead like Severin wanted for his father."

"I'm scared, Kelandra," Havyn said at last, his whole body shaking. Now that they'd crossed the border into Oscia, the old fears had crept back. Fear of the fists, the whips, and the boots. Havyn pressed a hand to his ribs, almost like he could feel them cracking again.

"Scared? Of the dead? There's nothing to fear from them, Havyn."

"Not them. Did you know I used to be a slave?"

She nodded. "Severin told me. I hope that hasn't upset you, I know it was your tale to tell if you wanted to."

"No, that's fine. That's not what I'm worried about. I'm scared the Oscians are going to make me a slave again. I don't want to go back to that, I don't."

"You won't have to, Havyn. I doubt they'd even recognise you as a slave now. I get the impression they didn't even know what their slaves looked like when they had them. You're a wizarding apprentice now, and you have the papers to prove it. No one will make you a slave. I won't allow it. They'll have to go through my sword first, and if I do say so myself, I am an excellent swordswoman." Kelandra smiled and ruffled his hair.

Havyn smiled. Kelandra had a way of making him feel better without even trying. "Thank you. I'm sorry if I seemed foolish."

"Havyn, there's nothing foolish about being scared. I get scared too sometimes, but that's what keeps me sharp."

"I'm sorry about what I said. About girl warriors. You're a match for any warrior I've ever seen."

"I take it there aren't any girl warriors in Oscia?" asked Kelandra, her eyes darting to the trees.

"Not that I know of—"

"Sssh! Did you hear something?"

Havyn shook his head, all he heard was the crackling of the fire and Ildar's snores, but he guessed that wasn't what Kelandra meant. "Wait here," Kelandra instructed. She shook Chayal awake while pressing her finger to her mouth. Chayal nodded and cocked his head as if listening for something. The Raven Warrior stood up to his full height. Watching him reminded Havyn of how short he was compared to the others. Both warriors drew their swords and stalked into the woods on silent feet. Havyn wondered how they could move so soundlessly.

A few minutes later, they stumbled back out. Kelandra was giggling so much she had to lean on Chayal's shoulders. "Just a rabbit," said Chayal. "Nothing to worry about."

By the time they'd returned, dawn painted the sky in a rosy hue, so Chayal woke Severin and Ildar so they could break their fast before making the rest of the journey to the Oscian capital. Havyn had never been to the city of Fair Haven, and he wondered how it would differ from Ravensfell, the capital of Arcathia.

"Severin, you're not eating," said Ildar, his brow furrowed.

"I'm not hungry." Severin looked into the distance.

"You've got to eat," insisted Ildar, holding out a plate of eggs and mushrooms to him.

Severin upended the plate. "I said I'm not hungry!" he roared.

The rest of them finished their meal in an uncomfortable silence.

Severin had sent all the horses and wagons back to Arcathia the night before, so after their meal, they made their way on foot. Severin and Chayal walked in front, Ildar and Havyn in the middle, and Kelandra took up position at the rear of their small party of travellers. Severin had yet to speak to Havyn after their altercation the night before, and if their eyes chanced to meet, Severin would quickly look away, his face flushed.

The journey didn't seem long, but it was wearying. There was nothing but trees on either side of them and a dirt path in front. Sometimes a colourful bird would swoop from the trees amid a rustle of leaves, but other than that, there was nothing to break the monotony. With the woods on both sides of them, there wasn't even a view of the sea from here. That was disappointing. Havyn liked to watch the waves. On a calm day, the waves lapping against the shore soothed him, and even when the sea was rough, he loved the sound as the waves crashed against the rocks. It filled him with an indescribable yearning for something, but he had no idea what.

"There," said Chayal, shielding his eyes from the sun and pointing to a high wooden fence in the distance. When they got closer, Havyn could see the fence was broken in places. Mounds of rubbish and human waste were piled up at lengths along the wooden city wall. Skeletal dogs nosed among them for scraps of food, growling and barking at each other. The air buzzed with flies, and the stench caused the group to gag when they neared the only gate. Havyn's heart thudded frantically against his chest as Chayal and Severin handed over their papers to the bearded guard.

The man barely looked at the papers before beckoning them through with a lazy wave of his hand. He didn't even spare a curious glance at Havyn, obviously too bored to take an interest in any of them.

"Prince Severin! Prince Severin!" a shrill voice called almost as soon as they were through. A fat, round man barrelled toward them, his whole face shining with perspiration. He was dressed from head to foot in folds of red velvet, though it was hard to tell whether the folds were the material or from the man's body. "We expected you yesterday. Is everything all right? Where's your retinue?"

"We were ambushed on the road," said Severin in a dull voice. "My father was killed."

Beneath the thick black beard, the man paled. "Your father? King Faran is dead?"

"You are?" asked Chayal, his hand hovering near his sword, Kelandra joined him, making sure they were both in front of Severin.

"Forgive me. I am Lord Joran, the chancellor. Please allow me to escort you all to your quarters. You must be fraught after such a journey. I will inform the king that you are here. There is a banquet tonight in the prince's honour. So sorry, in King Severin's honour."

"I haven't been crowned yet," said Severin.

"A formality, surely?" asked Lord Joran. "You are Arcathia's only legitimate heir. This way, we can go to the women's quarters first."

"None of us will be requiring the women's quarters," said Kelandra. "I am Severin's bodyguard, I stay with the king."

The chancellor stared at her. "But you cannot. It is forbidden. Men and women must be separate!"

"Kelandra, I will stay with Severin. We have to abide by our host's customs, don't we?" asked Chayal, smirking.

"Fine, but if one hair on his head comes to harm, Chayal, I am holding you personally responsible." Kelandra glowered at him.

Chayal laughed. "Oh, go and do some embroidery," he taunted her. Kelandra's face turned red with rage. Some of the Oscian ladies appeared to lead Kelandra away. Chayal had just had a lucky escape, Havyn was sure. "We'll see you at the banquet," said Chayal to Kelandra's retreating back. The chancellor wrung his hands.

"I take it we won't be seeing her at the banquet?" asked Ildar.

"No, women and men take their meals separately," said Lord Joran.

"So Severin won't meet his new bride tonight?"

The chancellor shivered, not meeting their eyes. "No, not tonight." Havyn sensed the man wasn't lying, but he was definitely hiding something.

Chapter Eleven

The accommodations at the castle in Fair Haven were a little better than the inn at Hammerfort, but only just. A large canopied bed with blue velvet curtains graced one wall. A chest rested at the foot of the bed, the wood scratched and misshapen from age. There were three pegs to hang clothes on, and a small table by one side of the bed. In deference to his royal status, Severin had been given a private bedchamber, but all of his companions had to share quarters with each other. Chayal had refused, insisting on staying in Severin's chamber.

"There's no telling what these Oscians might do," Chayal said. Severin wanted to be alone with his grief, but was too wrung out to argue with the bodyguard. Ildar and Havyn were in the next chamber, and unlike the inn, there was an actual bathroom between the two rooms. A tapestry hung on the wall behind Severin's bed, the material so faded and worn it was difficult to discern what the scene had once been, although Severin thought he saw a horse or two. There were cobwebs in each corner of the ceiling, waving with the breeze coming through the window hole.

The flagstone floor was uneven in places, and there wasn't even a rug to take the chill off the stones. There were no shutters or glass in the windows, just a gap in the wall. At least the bed linen looked clean enough, with a blue velvet coverlet embroidered with white flowers. The bed was big enough for two, but Severin inwardly sighed with relief when Chayal removed his bedroll from his pack and set it on the floor.

"It's a bit sparse, isn't it?" asked Chayal. "Looks like this room hasn't been used in years. You'd think they'd at least try to impress you."

"What would be the point? My father already signed the contract to wed me to Princess Ythrin. They don't need to impress me."

"Yes, but with your father dead, you might have decided to annul any contract between you. They have to know that it's now within your power to do so."

"If you believe the chancellor, they didn't know anything about it, so how could they know I might change my mind?"

"Are you going to? Change your mind, I mean."

Severin shrugged. He didn't want to discuss it. Chayal was taking the king's death rather well, as if it was just another incident that had happened.

"I'm going to have a bath," said Severin, nodding toward the other wooden door in the room. He needed some time on his own, and a bath would give him that opportunity. Severin didn't want to keep talking to Chayal about his father, princesses, or marriage. His mind was active enough already. Severin pushed the door open, but stopped short in surprise. He hadn't been the only one who'd thought of a bath.

The back of Havyn's head was visible while the young wizard lounged in the wooden tub. Severin glanced back into the bedchamber and saw that Chayal had his head down, settling in for a nap. The guard wasn't aware of Severin's spying. Severin knew he should turn and leave Havyn to his privacy, but his feet were stuck to the spot as he watched Havyn's arm lift out of the water and drip water from a sponge down onto his chest. Havyn sighed and did it again, his other arm somewhere beneath the water. Severin could see Havyn's elbow moving frantically up and down. Belatedly, Severin realised what he was seeing. He should turn away right now, but he couldn't.

Instead, Severin coughed. Havyn slid down in the bath, turning around and piercing Severin with his violet stare, his mouth agape. Severin had never seen anyone with eyes such a colour before. The bruising around his eye was fading now. Severin wondered dimly if Ildar had put some salve on it, and then wished he had been the one to rub the healing cream onto Havyn's skin. His fingers tingled with the wanting of it.

"Master Severin! I'm sorry. I didn't know you were there." Havyn placed his arms on the edge of the tub and leaned his head on them.

"I wanted a bath," said Severin, delighted to see the blush on Havyn's cheeks. His face and chest looked so smooth, so did his arms now that Severin noticed. Being so fair, Severin's own body hair was quite fine and light, but he'd expected Havyn to have hair as dark as that on his head, but the youth didn't seem to have any at all. Severin wished he could see into the water and see *all* of Havyn, but from his position at the door it was impossible, and he didn't want to make it obvious that he was looking. "I'm sorry, Havyn. I never meant you harm. You know that, don't you?"

"I know. I'm sorry about your father. That must have been so hard."

"It was," said Severin, realising that in all the commotion since his father had died, Havyn had been the only one who had offered him condolences.

"Can you turn around so I can get out and leave you to your bath?"

Severin nodded and turned, but as soon as he heard the water dripping from Havyn's body, he turned and saw Havyn from the rear. Sunlight flooded the room, making rainbows out of the water droplets that adorned Havyn's back and buttocks. It was like staring at one of the water nymphs out of the tales he'd been told as a child. Severin gasped. Guilt, grief, shame, and arousal warred within him. Severin choked back a sob as desire soared through his blood and made his staff throb.

Havyn turned at the noise, clutching the towel to his chest, the rest of it falling in folds to cover his stomach and thighs.

"Please," Severin gasped, taking a step forward, almost as if his feet were moving of their own volition. Severin's hand reached out to tug the towel away, his eyes never leaving Havyn's face. Havyn closed his eyes, inky eyelashes dusting his cheeks as he did so. Havyn's chest heaved. Severin knew his own breathing was just as erratic. Severin reached out to tug the towel from Havyn's body. Havyn's eyes glazed over, he gasped and arched his body toward Severin.

"Havyn, what's keeping you?" Ildar's voice from the doorway broke the spell they were under. Havyn yanked the towel tighter around his body, but couldn't hide the flush of his cheeks or the fact that his staff was at half-mast. "You'll be turning into a prune. Severin, I didn't see you there."

Severin dropped his hand at once, but wondered if Ildar had already seen what he'd been about to do.

"I came for a bath, but I didn't know anyone else was in here."

"Indeed," said Ildar. "We'll have to have some sort of system so it doesn't happen again, won't we? You should leave Havyn to get dressed now. I'll inform you when the bathroom's free."

Severin nodded and left, wondering what might have happened if the wizard hadn't interrupted when he did.

* * * *

After his bath—unfortunately alone, Severin dressed in his silver robes and swept his hair back before he and his companions made their way to the Great Hall of Fair Haven castle for the imminent banquet. When they passed servants in the hallways, Severin noticed that none of them were female. It seemed that this part of the castle had been reserved exclusively for males. He wondered how Kelandra was getting on, and hoped she would get a decent meal, even if it wasn't a banquet.

Two liveried servants opened the double doors when Severin, Chayal, Ildar, and Havyn approached. Inside by the flickering light of numerous torches, Severin could see acrobats tumbling over the floor, men eating fire, some eating their swords, and much to his surprise, women draped in shimmering fabrics danced for the entertainment of the guests seated at the tables that lined both sides of the hall. Some of the women were even sitting on the warrior's laps, their translucent outfits not hiding much as men nuzzled their necks and fondled them, not caring who might be watching.

On a raised dais, King Eltan sat on an ornately carved wooden throne. A red canopy with gold tassels hung above it. A tapestry bearing a black swan rested on the wall behind him. His hair was grey, including his beard, and his face was creased, mapping his life. A scar ran from his left eye to his jaw, testifying to his time as a warrior, nothing out of the ordinary for a king of Arcathia or Oscia. Severin wondered if the man had gained the scar in one of the many battles between their two nations, maybe even from Severin's father himself. At the thought of his father, Severin stamped down the ache, wishing things had been different.

The chancellor, still dressed in the clothes he'd been wearing earlier, whispered something to Eltan, who looked at the foursome by the door. He lifted his right hand, every finger was adorned with a jewelled ring, but his clothes were plain, even if well made.

"Come," said Eltan, beckoning them forward with a click of his fingers. Severin bristled at being addressed as if he was no more than a servant. He marched forward with purposeful strides. Once they reached the king, Ildar and the others sank to one knee, but Severin remained standing. He was a king now too, of the same rank as the man before him—he refused to bow.

There was an empty stool next to the king's throne, Eltan waved Severin into it. Chayal moved into place behind him so he could taste the food first. There were platters of various meats and breads arranged on the table in front of him, most of it swimming in grease.

Severin's stomach lurched. The fare didn't seem much of an improvement than what they'd gotten at the terrible inn where they'd stayed. Ildar and Havyn made their way to the table closest to the dais. Among the leather-clad, brawny warriors, they looked like tropical birds forced into a hen coop.

A small page appeared by Severin's elbow and poured out a hefty measure of wine into the pewter goblet. Severin lifted the goblet to his lips, but Chayal plucked it from his hands. "You know better than that, Sire," he said. The man took a sip, then he set the goblet down and nodded to Severin.

"You do not trust my Hall?" demanded Eltan.

"We were ambushed and King Faran murdered," said Chayal. "There's trust, and then there's blind stupidity. They were Oscian arrows."

"How dare you accuse us of such treachery! We want peace. We had nothing to do with King Faran's murder!"

"Havyn," Severin called. "Come here."

King Eltan watched in bemusement while Havyn made his way up to the dais and bowed on one knee, his hair fell forward, hiding his face.

"Is it the truth?" asked Severin.

"It is, Sire. He doesn't know anything about what happened to your father."

"What's this? A Truth Seeker? You brought a Truth Seeker into my Hall without my permission?"

"He is part of my retinue, I don't need your permission," said Severin firmly.

"You flout the rules of hospitality with impunity, King Severin, but I must admit that I admire someone with spirit. There have been few who have ever stood up to me. I know now you are the best man for the job."

"What job?"

"Your bride has been abducted," said Eltan. "You'll have to find her before you can marry her."

Chapter Twelve

W hat do you mean 'abducted'?" asked Severin, wondering what other revelations he was expected to cope with. Since he'd reached his majority, life had gotten weirder and weirder. Not only was he expected to marry a princess he had never met, but now he'd discovered she wasn't even here.

"I thought that was obvious, Severin. Princess Ythrin has been kidnapped. She needs to be found before the marriage can proceed. Find her and bring her back, this is what I ask of you."

"Do you know who's taken her? Has there been a ransom?"

"No, no ransom, but I have my suspicions." Eltan sipped from his own goblet, and then wiped his mouth on his sleeve.

"They are?"

"Lately she has been making sojourns with her ladies to a fortune-teller. This woman has been flouting the law for years now, but since she is not Oscian, we cannot arrest her."

"So you do not allow fortune-telling in Oscia?"

"No, that's allowed. But this woman lives with her son, and that is against the law for Oscians. I don't know what land she comes from, but she makes a great show of flouting the fact that she can live with a male while the Oscians can't. I don't want a rebellion on my hands because of her."

"You think this woman has taken Princess Ythrin for ransom?"

"No, not her. I think her son has kidnapped Ythrin. He hasn't been seen since she disappeared either. You and your Truth Seeker are perhaps just what we need. You can go to her, demand that she tell you the truth. I want my niece back," said Eltan.

"May we speak in private, King Eltan?" asked Severin, noticing that a lot of the warriors now watched them with interest.

Eltan nodded, speaking to Lord Joran, and then indicating that Severin and Chayal should follow him to a private chamber behind the dais. The room was bare except for an unlit fireplace. There were no tapestries on the walls, not even rushes for the floor. The room had a chill, damp feeling.

"It was my father who signed the contract arranging my marriage to Ythrin," said Severin. "If you still wish for me to marry your niece, I want to re-negotiate."

"Oh, now I see. You want to bring us to war again, do you? I've had enough of war, Severin. I'm dying. In my last battle, I took a wound that has festered. I don't have much time left. I wanted to see Ythrin married before I go. I also had a desire to see things between our nations settled. There has been too much bloodshed in my lifetime. I am committed to bringing peace between us—to reuniting these two kingdoms once more."

"I want the same things," said Severin. "You know I'm no warrior, but I want to be a good king to all my people, Oscians and Arcathians alike. I want you to change the laws about banning marriage for everyone. I know you made an exception for Ythrin and me, but everyone should be free to marry whom and when they choose. Change the law before you die so they'll know their king was just. Let men and women be free to love once again. There were female dancers in the Hall tonight, why were they allowed?"

"That's different, they're slaves," said Eltan. "They aren't women."

Severin shuddered. "I want slavery abolished," added Severin.

"What? No, that cannot be done! What will their owners do without workers for their fields and houses?"

"If they want workers, they can pay them a fair price like every civilised nation does," retorted Severin. "These are my terms."

"If I agree to this, you will look for Ythrin and marry her? There will be peace between us again?"

"There will," said Severin. "I swear on my honour."

"You could just change the laws yourself when I die and you become King of Oscia," said Eltan.

"I could, but wouldn't you prefer to be remembered for doing something good?"

"I'm not sure the slave traders will agree," said Eltan.

"There are more slaves than traders, are there not? Free them, and you will have even more loyal subjects."

"Or once free, they could all rise up and attack us."

"That is indeed a risk. Are you willing to take it?" asked Severin.

"You drive a hard bargain, Severin, but I agree to those terms. Lord Joran, see that the statutes are amended and make an announcement to all the governors. Send messengers throughout

Oscia that the ban is lifted, and henceforth all slaves in Oscia are free men and women, they are to be treated accordingly."

Joran beamed at his king. "It shall be as you command, Sire. This is a good thing, a very good thing."

* * * *

The next morning, after a breakfast of thin broth and watered down wine, King Eltan showed them a crude map and pointed out the fortune-teller's house. Her name was Lamil and she lived in the middle of the merchant's quarter. Fair Haven was a city divided into four distinct areas, the harbour area, which included warehouses, taverns, and a few other entertainment houses, including brothels and gambling dens. Then there was the castle along with its surrounds, which included the more well to do houses and a few upmarket shops. Next to the merchant's quarter was where everyone else ended up—those too poor to afford more luxurious accommodations so they lived in whatever shelter was available, whether that was a wooden shack or a cloak thrown over sticks.

As they passed through the poorer section of the city, the stench of rotting vegetables, spoiled meat, and other odours got stronger. Severin hadn't eaten much breakfast, but if he had, it wouldn't have surprised him if it had decided to make a reappearance at all the conflicting smells assailing his nostrils. Ragged children dashed about, playing with each other, and baiting snarling, hungry dogs. The children and the animals looked like they'd missed quite a few meals. Severin wondered how things had ever got to such a state. He turned to Kelandra and whispered in her ear.

Kelandra nodded at his request, then found a group of children and handed a couple of pennies to each of them. It was too risky to pass out gold because that would have made them a more obvious target for thieves and pick-pockets, but a few pennies given in charity shouldn't arouse too many suspicions of their wealth.

Ildar stopped at a wooden door with a drawing of a circle scratched into it. There were no visible windows on any of the buildings, and the only indication of what each shop was selling were the signs hanging over their doorways. But at the door where Ildar stopped, there was no sign. The building had a shabby, worn look. The paint peeled away in brown flecks, showing the green underneath, and the roof was bowing, with a few tiles missing and even more broken.

"This is it," Ildar said to Severin. "The circle is their sign."

Apart from the Oracle at the temple, Severin had never had much experience with fortune tellers, but that had never been considered trade. It seemed strange to pay to get your fortune told. Ildar rapped on the door with his staff. Severin and the others shuffled their feet while they waited for an answer.

A few moments later, a middle-aged woman flung the door open, her face creased with worry. A multi-coloured scarf covered her hair so it was difficult to discern what colour it was, but her eyes were so dark they looked black. Like Kelandra, she wasn't wearing a gown, but a pair of leather breeches and a red silk shirt with black buttons down the front.

"Mistress Lamil?" enquired Ildar. "Lamil the fortune-teller?"

"Yes, what of it?"

"My name is Ildar. I am a wizard, and this is my Master, Severin. May we come in?"

"A wizard?" The woman glanced at Havyn. "And a Truth Seeker, too? Come in, come in." The woman stood aside so they could enter the house. In contrast to the shabby exterior, the hallway was well decorated with fresh white paint. Despite the lack of windows, it seemed bright, but Severin couldn't see any visible lighting anywhere.

Lamil ushered them into some sort of parlour where there were red velvet sofas and hard back chairs along with three circular tables, all draped in red cloth. Crystal balls sat on one, decks of tarot cards on another, and one was covered with rune tiles.

"I knew you were coming," said Lamil, sitting down at the table next to the runes. "I suppose King Eltan sent you, spouting more of his lies?" She waved Havyn into the chair opposite her, and then invited the others to sit where they would.

"Lies, Mistress?" asked Havyn, taking the seat.

"My Aviel would never harm a hair on Princess Ythrin's head," she said vehemently. "He worships the ground that girl walks on."

"Yet, both of them are indeed missing," chimed in Ildar.

"Yes, but that doesn't mean anything. They could have eloped."

Chayal laughed. "A princess and a fortune-teller's son? That's so likely, isn't it?"

"Chayal!" Ildar chided. "Love knows no boundaries of class, it *is* a possibility we must consider. I understand the princess came to consult you often?"

"She did, but it wasn't her fortune she wanted told, it was his," Lamil jerked a thumb in Severin's direction. "Ythrin said she'd been having dreams about the prince from Arcathia."

"My fortune? She was dreaming about me?"

"Well, that's what she said. I couldn't get any more out of her, she didn't remember much about the dreams when she woke."

"Is it usual in Oscia to have prophetic dreams?" asked Ildar, leaning forward, his whole face agog.

"Not usual, no, but it's in the royal blood, isn't it? Ythrin's mother was Aldari like Eltan's wife."

"Aldari? Are you sure?" asked Ildar.

"Of course I'm bloody sure. You can't mistake Aldari for anything else, can you? Like angels, both of them were. So beautiful to look at it hurt the eyes. And you." Lamil turned back to Havyn. She cupped his face in her hand, turning his head this way and that. "Aldari blood is strong in you. Who was your father?"

"I don't know. I'm an orphan. I never knew my parents."

"Such a shame. The Aldari don't live long once they've left their Sanctuary, that's probably what happened to your mother or father."

"You think my parents were Aldari?" Havyn asked. The hope in his voice almost broke Severin's heart.

"One of them at least. If you were full Aldari, you wouldn't have survived this long."

"Mistress, what can you tell us about Princess Ythrin's visits with regards to Severin's fortunes?" asked Ildar.

"Not a lot really. I had never met Severin. In order to read his future, I would have needed to meet him. It was no good just knowing his name. The princess wasn't convinced, so she returned time and again, but I was unable to help her."

"And your son was here? So they could have fallen in love?" Ildar continued. "Were they ever left alone? Is there a chance she could be pregnant?"

"Not while they were here. Ythrin's women were always with her, and I was always in the room, but Aviel did go out on his own quite a bit. Perhaps they met up in secret. I just don't know."

Havyn nodded to Ildar. "It's the truth as she sees it."

"If they eloped, have you any idea where they might have gone?" asked Severin, wondering what would happen if the two of them had indeed run off and gotten married. How would that leave Oscia and Arcathia then?

"They may have gone across the sea to Sadea. My brother lives there, and there is no law banning marriage. It is where a lot of lovers have gone."

"Do you know where in Sadea?"

"A town called Aldford. My brother lives near the river, he's the miller there."

"We'll need a boat," said Chayal.

"And supplies," added Kelandra. "Not to mention a captain. None of us are sailors."

"Please, I beg you," said Lamil. "Find them and bring them home."

"We will do our best," said Severin, surprised to find he meant it.

Chapter Thirteen

Havyn absently kicked a stone along in front of him as he and Ildar made their way back to the castle. Severin, Chayal, and Kelandra had decided to leave Havyn and Ildar behind while they sought passage on a ship. They didn't need all five of them to speak to the captain, so they would meet Ildar and Havyn later for the journey. The fortune-teller's words were uppermost in his mind. He was half-Aldari. One half of that legendary race. He wondered if he had actually dreamed it.

"Did she upset you?" Ildar asked gently. "The fortune-teller?"

"No. I don't know," replied Havyn. "If I really am half-Aldari, why couldn't I use my magic to escape from being a slave? Why did I allow all those Masters to mistreat me?"

Ildar pulled Havyn aside and stooped a little so that they were eye to eye. "Havyn, lad, you didn't know you were Aldari or a wizard. You didn't know you had magic so how could you have used it to save you? Do you think a baby is born knowing how to walk and talk? No, they have to be taught these things. It's the same with wizards. They have to learn how to use their power. A baby is born with a tongue and with legs, but they need to learn how to use them. You did nothing wrong, Havyn. They may have hurt you, beat you, and whipped you, but you're still alive. You survived and that is something none of them can take away from you."

Tears dripped down his face, he tried to turn, but Ildar pulled him close and hugged him to his chest, letting Havyn cry it out. Everything was such a muddle—his feelings for Severin, his heritage and newly discovered magic, the desire to please Ildar, and yet despairing that he would only ever be a disappointment. He no longer knew what to think or feel. It was all so confusing.

"Hush, lad, hush." Ildar stroked his back. "It'll be all right. You'll see." They fell silent for a moment, Ildar rocking him like a child. "You'll see."

Havyn didn't know how long he cried in Ildar's arms, but soon they were gathering quite an audience of curious looking children. "Let's get you back to the castle," said Ildar briskly, not allowing him to wallow any more. Havyn nodded and wiped his eyes. He felt a bit better now that he had cried, but he didn't think it was something he wanted to make a habit of. Men didn't cry, as his cruel masters had often taunted him when they punished him with the whip or their boots.

Once they were back in the chamber they shared, Ildar took out some of his books and drilled Havyn on his magical studies. Havyn sat cross-legged on the floor while Ildar sat on the edge of the bed with his legs dangling over the sides.

"What's a Dreamer?" asked Ildar.

"A Dreamer is a wizard who can tell the future from their dreams, which are called True Imaginings."

"What is the Oracle?"

"The Oracle is a conduit. She can help people who don't normally have True Imaginings to see their future paths."

"Why are many paths shown?"

"Because the future can change depending on your choices."

"Very good, Havyn. I thought we'd practice some summoning spells now, I think you're ready. I want you to call the bolster into your hand."

"How?"

"Just think of how much you want that pillow in your hand."

"Aren't there any magic words to the spell?"

"No. But if you want to say something to help you focus, you can."

Havyn nodded, looking behind Ildar at the cushions piled on the bed. He didn't feel very magical at the moment, and his gaze wandered to Ildar's staff. Wouldn't Havyn need one of those in order to do magic? Ildar didn't seem to think so, in fact, he seemed confident that Havyn could summon the pillow with nothing but his will. Havyn sat up straighter, not wanting to disappoint his mentor. Havyn imagined the pride he'd see on Ildar's face once he'd retrieved the bolster. The vision made him smile. Havyn held out his arms, already feeling the weight of the pillow in them. For a few moments, nothing happened, but then the pillow lurched and tumbled the length of the bed before flopping down onto the floor like a fish.

"Not bad for your first try," said Ildar. "Do it again."

Havyn tried summoning the cushions again and again, but for a long time he could only make them tumble off the bed rather than fly from it and land in his hands. Ildar didn't seem to think this was unusual and even seemed pleased with Havyn's progress. "Once more, then," said Ildar, standing up and folding his arms over his chest.

Not expecting to succeed, Havyn lifted his arms out like before. This time, one of the pillows rose into the air and flew toward Havyn like a leaf buffeted by the wind. The force of the pillow slamming into him almost made him lose his balance. He turned to grin at Ildar.

"Well done, Havyn. Shall I let you into a little secret?"

"A secret?" asked Havyn.

"Yes. You could have done that much sooner if I hadn't been sitting on the bed. Every time you tried to call a pillow to you, you weren't just dealing with the weight of a feather pillow. You were dealing with my weight too. That's why the pillows were moving so sluggishly. I was surprised you got them to move at all. You have enormous potential, Havyn. I've never met a more powerful wizard than you."

"Really?"

"Indeed. Do you remember what we discussed? That a wizard needs to remain pure in order to better channel his power."

Heat rose to Havyn's cheeks, remembering what Ildar had seen in the bathroom. "Nothing happened, I swear."

"I know, Havyn. But what might have happened if I hadn't been there? I trust you, but I'm not so sure about Severin. He has a way of always getting what he wants. Right now, he has set his sights on you."

"I'm sorry," said Havyn, miserable that he'd disappointed Ildar.

"I'm not angry at you, Havyn. I know you're young, and it feels like you're denying yourself what every other young man and woman wants more than anything, but power isn't gained without sacrifice. I know that." Ildar coughed delicately. "The body sometimes makes demands on you, but you must resist them. Every time you spill your seed, your power decreases."

"So I can't even..." Havyn waved his hands around his groin. "Touch myself?"

"No, not like that. I know it's difficult, Havyn, but it will be worth it, won't it?"

"Yes, sir," Havyn replied, but even to himself it sounded like a lie.

* * * *

Three days later, all five of them were on their way to the harbor, the others having secured passage. Havyn was used to travel. Sometimes, he'd been with one Master for just a few weeks at a time before he was sold on again, but he had never crossed the sea. In fact, he'd never been on a boat at all. He stared in awe at the ships moored at the docks, their white sails rippling with the wind. Gulls wheeled overhead, swooping down to snatch food out of unwary people's hands. Seeing them close up, Havyn realised how large the birds were.

The ship they were to sail on was called *Calira*. Havyn wondered who it was named for—the captain's mother, sister, or sweetheart? A man almost as broad as he was tall marched down the wooden gangplank with the air of someone who was master of all he surveyed. He looked the party up and down. His eyes raked over Kelandra the most, and Havyn was surprised to find that Kelandra blushed at the scrutiny. He had never seen Kelandra show an interest in anyone of the opposite sex before.

"This is Captain Kanmor," said Chayal as he introduced Ildar and Havyn. Kanmor was dressed in a pair of black leather trousers, but he was bare to the waist. A pelt of russet hair covered his chest, but he was as beardless as an Arcathian. His hair, a rich hue of autumn leaves, was long and thick. He tied it back in a ponytail which hung to his waist. The muscles on his arms and chest rippled with every movement. Havyn could see why Kelandra had seemed a bit flustered by their handsome captain. He was a little flustered himself, especially when the captain shook hands with him, and his hazel eyes seemed to see right down to Havyn's very soul.

"Havyn, help me with the luggage," instructed Ildar, even though Havyn knew the wizard was capable of carrying the pack by himself. After their talks, it was obvious that Ildar was trying to save Havyn from himself. But what if Havyn didn't want to be saved? What if he wanted what he knew the glint in Kanmor's eyes offered? Out of the corner of his eye, Havyn saw Severin glaring at both of them. Havyn's heart jumped at the waves of jealousy he sensed coming from the young king.

"Let me show you to your quarters," said Kanmor, hooking his arm through Kelandra's and ushering her up the gangplank. Kelandra blushed and tittered, reminding Havyn so much of Lady Kessarie in that moment he had to stifle a chuckle.

"You'd better watch out, Severin, or you'll lose one of the Daughters to home and hearth," guffawed Chayal.

"I don't think the captain is particularly interested in that," said Ildar. "So much as he is interested in bedding everything that moves."

"Ildar!" chided Severin. "There's no need to be coarse. Kelandra would never fall for that."

"So says the naïve virgin." Chayal laughed again. Severin blushed and Havyn's cheeks heated.

Havyn picked up Ildar's pack, hefted it over his shoulder, and walked onto the ship. Sailors prepared the vessel, hoisting up sails, pulling on ropes, and consulting charts. The whole deck buzzed with activity.

"Saleth," Captain Kanmor called to one of the nearby sailors. "Show our guests to their quarters, will you? After that, make sure that all the supplies are on board so we can set sail."

"Aye, aye, sir," said Saleth, a young man around Havyn's age with short brown hair peeking out from a woollen cap. His eyes were as blue as the sea around them. He winked at Havyn as the captain sauntered off to do whatever it was captains did. "This way, gents," said Saleth, leading them down the steps that led into the bowels of the ship.

"We don't have much space so it's two to a cabin, except for Lady Kelandra," said the youth with a sigh. "She's very pretty, isn't she?"

"Don't get your hopes up, lad," said Chayal. "That one's married to her sword."

"Typical," said Saleth, but he didn't sound too disappointed.

Beneath the deck, there was a narrow corridor lined on both sides with doors and a wooden handrail about waist high. Anchored in the harbour, there wasn't much movement, but already Havyn legs began to sway. Saleth pushed open the first door. "Your cabin, Lord Severin," he said as Severin and Chayal peered over his shoulder.

"Bottom or top bunk?" Chayal asked with a grin and a wink at Severin. Havyn was surprised to find Severin blush at the question before answering. "Top."

Saleth pushed the next door open so that Havyn and Ildar could see their cabin. It was the same size and layout as Severin and Chayal's cabin. Two bunks attached firmly to the wooden walls, and there was a small space on the floor with just enough room for them to stand before getting into the beds.

"See you at dinner, gents," said Saleth before he left to see to his other duties.

"Sir," Havyn began. "Why did Severin blush about which bed he wanted?"

When Ildar explained it to him, Havyn's face heated with embarrassment. Did people really do that? When Ildar offered Havyn the first choice of bunks, he hesitated for a moment before, with a hot face, he claimed the bottom one.

Chapter Fourteen

For the first few days at sea, Severin and Havyn were laid low with seasickness. Despite never having been on a ship before, Kelandra, Chayal, and Ildar all seemed to find their sea legs at once. Ildar spent his time in the galley helping the cook prepare flasks of ginger tea for them, which he made them drink sitting up on the deck.

"You'll feel worse cooped up in your cabin," Ildar warned the two young men who sat huddled in blankets at the prow of the boat, shivering when sea spray washed over them. Severin was almost sure Ildar wanted them on deck so he'd know exactly where they were. Ildar was worse than some of the chaperones for the ladies back at the palace. Severin understood. Ildar was just looking after his apprentice, but sometimes it was frustrating. Feeling so ill, Severin hadn't been in the mood for any amorous adventures anyway, but about a week after they'd been at sea, that changed.

The seasickness was completely gone. He could spend time watching the waves now, and when Ildar wasn't looking, he watched Havyn too. Havyn was thinner again, so was Severin because neither of them had been able to keep any food down for a while. It was a few days after Severin's own recovery before Havyn began to feel more like himself, and much to Severin's chagrin, Ildar spent a lot of time with Havyn in their cabin, keeping up with Havyn's studies.

Out of necessity, they all shared close quarters because the ship was so small privacy was non-existent. Sometimes Severin lay in his bunk for hours, his staff throbbing between his legs when he thought of the thin wall separating him from Havyn. Every time he closed his eyes, he saw Havyn as he'd been when he'd just emerged from the bath, and that only made his need worse. It couldn't be assuaged though. Chayal was in the bunk beneath him, and any time Severin moved, the bed creaked like an unoiled door. He just had to grit his teeth and bear it.

Ildar never left Havyn alone for any length of time. At first, Severin was convinced that Ildar didn't want Severin anywhere near his apprentice, but then he realised Ildar seemed keener on protecting Havyn from their captain. Ildar had no such qualms about allowing Captain Kanmor and Kelandra to be alone together, but then Kelandra wasn't Ildar's responsibility. Severin took it upon himself to act as her big brother despite the fact that Kelandra was five years older than him, and he thwarted the captain's advances when he could.

This did nothing except annoy her, and she cornered Severin one day as he gazed at the waves, watching the frothy foam while the ship slid through the water.

"I can look after myself, Severin!" she insisted. "I don't need you acting like my mother."

"The captain is a lot bigger than you," Severin pointed out. "What if he tried something?"

"He's just flirting," Kelandra said. "He doesn't really want me. It's Havyn he's after. The man spends more time talking about him than trying to get me out of my clothes."

"He's been trying to get you out of your clothes?" demanded Severin, reaching for a sword that was no longer at his hip.

"Of course not! Just a turn of phrase. He's a charmer, I know that. I'm not as foolish as the Court, Severin. Yes, I was flattered by his attention, but he is not interested in me, and I have no intention of letting flattery go to my head. I take my duties and my vows seriously."

"Is he really after Havyn?" asked Severin, more worried about the young apprentice than he cared to admit.

"Yes, hadn't you noticed?"

"I thought I was imagining it. Jealous."

"Ildar thinks so too. Haven't you noticed he hasn't let Havyn out of his sight?" asked Kelandra, glancing around to where Ildar and Havyn were perusing some books. Chayal was with the captain by the wheelhouse, overseeing some charts.

"How long do you think it will be before we get to Sadea?"

"I hope it's soon," said Kelandra. "As I said, I can look after myself, but what about Havyn? What if the captain gets him on his own one night?"

"We'll just have to make sure that never happens," said Severin firmly. The thought of that man pawing at Havyn just couldn't be borne. Havyn was *his*, no matter what foolish notions about magic and sex Ildar had been filling his apprentice's head with.

"Land ahoy!" one of the sailors called from the crow's nest. Severin looked to the distant horizon. Sure enough, he could see the outline of mountains rising from the depths of the sea. The land still looked far away though, and Severin collared Saleth, the young sailor, as he went by.

"How long until we reach shore?" asked Severin.

Saleth held his hand to his eyes and squinted. "Maybe a day or two." A day or two. Another few days to make sure Captain Kanmor went nowhere near Havyn. A few more days with no privacy. He could cope with it, he hoped.

* * * *

On their last evening aboard the ship, Severin was on his bunk with his head behind his hands, listening to Chayal sharpen his sword. Severin supposed he ought to be doing the same with his own, but he really wasn't in the mood to look after his weapons. For a few days now, Chayal had seemed as if he wanted to talk to Severin about something of some import, but either they were interrupted or Chayal couldn't say what was on his mind.

"Out with it, Chayal," Severin said. The need to know had been gnawing at him for days. "What did you want to say to me?"

"Sire?" Chayal didn't even look up.

"Tell me what you wish me to know."

"It's about your father, Severin. I wasn't sure how to broach the subject. You were so upset that he never said he loved you. I know he loved you; it was obvious in his words and tone. He hardly ever spoke about anything else but you. He was harder on you than anyone else because he didn't want you to make the same mistakes. King Faran understood you a lot better than he ever let on."

"What do you mean?" Severin rested his elbows on his bunk and leaned over to look at Chayal.

"Faran was like you. His father wasn't so understanding when he caught Faran with a lover, and the wedding to your mother was arranged within a matter of weeks."

"Lover? A male lover?" Severin could hardly believe it. His father had never mentioned anything to him. There had been no inkling that they had shared this secret all these years, but he could think of no reason why Chayal would lie about it.

When someone knocked on the door, Chayal answered it and their conversation was cut short. From the small sliver of open doorway, Severin saw Saleth standing there with a lantern in his hand.

"Yes?" asked Chayal

"You're all invited to dinner at the captain's table," said Saleth. "This will probably be your last night aboard with us."

"Thank you, Saleth. We will be up presently," said Severn, swinging his legs down and hopping to the floor from the top bunk.

"Last night on board," said Chayal. "Thank the Raven! I can't wait to get back to dry land. If I see another ship's biscuit, I shall scream."

Severin tried not to laugh. Chayal had not been enamoured of the ship's food so far, but perhaps a dinner with the captain would change that. Severin couldn't imagine the captain eating the same rations as the other sailors. He waited until Chayal exited the cabin before standing up himself because there wasn't much room with both of them there. Their clothes were a bit wrinkled and travel worn, but since they had no way of changing that, they would have to do.

When Severin exited the cabin, the ship lurched to one side. He ended up bumping into Havyn and Ildar who were just emerging from their cabin at the same time. Severin held on to Havyn longer than was warranted, using the excuse of the ship's rocking while he steadied both of them. Havyn wouldn't look at him, and Ildar yanked hard on the boy's arm, hurrying him along to the ladder that led to the deck.

Severin sighed, wondering if he would ever get Havyn alone, then he wondered if he was any better than the captain, who appeared to want the exact same thing. Ildar seemed to have Havyn on a very tight leash. The wizard interrupted at the most awkward moments, and Severin wondered if Ildar had put some sort of spell on his apprentice to protect his virtue.

The captain waited by his open cabin door and smiled at their approach. Severin pulled up short when he saw Kelandra. He'd never seen her like this before. Instead of Kelandra the warrior, she was definitely Kelandra the young woman. The breeches and tunic were gone, and instead, she wore a gown of sea blue with long, full sleeves and a train that trailed along behind her. Her hair was swept up in some sort of arrangement that made her neck seem even longer and drew one's gaze to the swell of her bosom. Severin stared at her in surprise—Kelandra had cleavage?

Captain Kanmor couldn't seem to take his gaze off her. As Kelandra reached him, he bowed low, and then took Kelandra's right hand in his and bestowed a kiss on the back of it.

"Welcome," said the captain, standing aside so they could enter the room. There was a table with eight chairs in the middle of the room, all of them bolted to the floor. There were pewter plates and goblets, all somehow stuck to the table too, but the cutlery was sliding this way and that with the swell of the sea.

"Kelandra, you shall sit next to me," said Kanmor.

When Kelandra passed Severin, she winked at him. Severin realised his friend was trying to take the captain's mind off Havyn and it appeared to be working. It seemed the captain was one of those who could take pleasure in either the male or the female form.

They all found their places, Ildar in the middle between Severin and Havyn, Chayal on Severin's other side next to Kelandra and the rest of the places empty. Candles in glass lanterns swung on the wall as the ship rocked, casting strange shadows on the hardwood floors. Once everyone was seated, Kanmor clapped his hands and Saleth emerged from a hidden doorway. The man poured everyone a measure of wine into the goblets. Despite the lad's best efforts, quite a bit of the wine sloshed over the sides and dribbled down the table onto the floor. There was very little water to be had on sea voyages as Severin discovered in the few weeks they'd been aboard. It was difficult to keep it fresh, so most liquid had been in the form of wine or ale.

Once he'd finished that, Saleth disappeared again, and then returned with their first course—some sort of filleted fish, which was overly salted, but nearly everything had been salted to preserve it. The fish was on a plate of its own, which Saleth set down on the bolted plate, so to eat it, one had to keep hold of it, and otherwise the plate would slide off the table. Severin washed it down with a swig of wine and wondered if everyone else saw double yet. It was one of the strongest wines he'd ever tasted.

"How far is it to Aldford?" asked Chayal as he licked his fingers after finishing his fish.

"About a day's ride from the harbour at Beren," said Captain Kanmor, still staring, obviously enraptured at Kelandra. "Just follow the river up and you'll get there. The river starts out broad at the estuary, but it gets narrower the further inland you go, otherwise we could have sailed the ship straight there."

"A days' ride, you say?" asked Ildar. "Are there horses to hire in Beren?"

Kanmor laughed. "Of course. You can hire anything in Beren if you have the gold."

Severin was aware that all eyes turned to Havyn at that statement. The youth flushed and stared at the floor.

"Thank you, Captain," said Severin.

"You're welcome. We don't usually get very many passengers. It was a treat to have you all on board. Just be careful when you get to Sadea."

"Why?"

"This is an Oscian ship. The Sadeans have no love of Oscians."

"You don't look very Oscian, Captain," said Kelandra.

"No. I'm not," said Kanmor, but he didn't elaborate further.

When Saleth arrived with their main course, a whole peacock cooked and stuffed with chestnuts, the conversation turned to food and wine, but Severin couldn't help wondering what the Oscians had done to Sadea.

Chapter Fifteen

When the ship sailed into the harbour at Beren, Havyn stood by the railing at the side of the ship and stared fascinated at all the industry taking place there. Sailors unpacked barrels, bolts of cloth, trays of glassware, sacks of grain or meal, bottles of spices, vials of medicine, and of course, the recently caught fish. There were hundreds of ships all bobbing at anchor while their wares were unpacked. People called to each other in many different languages and wore different styles of clothes. Warehouses lined the far side of the harbour, and in front of them, market stalls were set up. Despite the early hour, all of the businesses were busy with prospective purchasers. Havyn had never seen anything like it.

"How are you feeling now, Havyn?" Kelandra asked once she joined him by the railing.

"Much better, thank you. But I'll be glad to get off the boat."

"I think we all will," she replied, placing a hand on his shoulder and squeezing it. In a few moments, their mooring was getting closer, and ropes were thrown to a few boys ashore, who deftly tied them around black stumps that protruded from the concrete. Havyn had no idea what they were called, but they probably had some seafaring name. Between the warehouses, a river ribboned off into the distance. Havyn supposed this was the one they were supposed to follow to Aldford.

Once the ship was tied and the gangplank down, Captain Kanmor appeared to lead them all down, taking Kelandra's hand and kissing her wrist before he returned to his ship and they set off to find the ostler. Beren was a maze of streets and alleyways that criss-crossed each other, although the streets themselves were clean and there were no beggars that they could see. The buildings were well-maintained, no peeling paint or cracks in the plaster.

Ildar kept close to Havyn, and despite liking his mentor, Havyn wanted a rest from the wizard. Cooped up with him in the tiny cabin for the past few weeks had made him long for his own bedroom back at the palace where he could be alone whenever he wanted. That hadn't been possible aboard the ship.

"Chayal, do we have enough to hire three horses?" asked Severin. Havyn glanced at the young king.

"There should be enough, my lord," said Chayal. While they travelled, Severin would pretend to be a lord, not a king. They'd decided it would be safer that way. It was obvious he wasn't any sort of peasant. His bearing would give away his noble status, and Severin was not very good at subterfuge. A lord travelling with a couple of servants and a wizard would not seem out of place, but Chayal and Ildar both reckoned the less people who knew Severin was now the king, the better. Bandits might expect a high ransom for a king, but lords were so plentiful on the road that they probably wouldn't kidnap them; however, robbery was still a real threat.

They smelled the stables before they reached them, and Havyn had to swallow a few times to ease the nausea at the smell of horse, hay, and waste. It had been a while since he'd cleaned out stables.

Chayal talked to the ostler, a small man with a thin black moustache and a head as bald as an egg. The sun glinted off his pate every time he moved suddenly, which was quite often. Havyn wondered if he had some sort of illness that made him move so jerkily. It was like he couldn't quite control any of his limbs.

Around an hour later, Chayal returned leading three horses by the reins. There was a large black stallion, a bay mare, and a grey mare. All three seemed enormous to Havyn who'd never been on a horse before.

"Havyn, since you are not an experienced rider, you will be with me," said Severin while he checked the saddle and stirrups. "Ildar, for the same reason, you'll be with Chayal."

Ildar tried to protest, but Severin cut him off. "We don't have time to argue. The sooner we get to Aldford, the better." Severin climbed up on the horse with grace that Havyn knew he'd never be able to match. Kelandra found a box that Ildar could stand on to reach the stallion Chayal had appropriated, and then brought it over so Havyn could use it as a boost too.

Havyn stood on the box and Severin leaned down to offer him his hand. A few moments later, Havyn was sitting astride his first horse, Severin's arms holding him securely about the waist. "Just hold on to her mane or her reins," advised Severin. "We don't want you falling off, do we?" asked Severin, very close to Havyn's ear. Havyn shivered, although he was far from cold. He still hadn't forgotten that day in the bath when Severin had pleaded with him for something Havyn couldn't give. Not if he wanted to remain a wizard. But sometimes, especially at night when he had been lying alone in his cabin bunk, he couldn't stop thinking about Severin only a wall away. He wondered what would happen if they gave in to their desires.

Severin gave the horse a gentle press to the flanks, and then they were off, trotting along the city streets. There were no walls here, no guards, just a road that followed the river out into the countryside. The trees were sparser here than in Arcathia and Oscia, most were shorter too, and most of the plant life they saw was small. Once away from the city, the riders set the horses to galloping, and Havyn had to hold on with white knuckled hands, afraid he would go tumbling off. Severin had a good grip on his waist though, and Havyn found he quite liked being held in Severin's arms. For a while, he allowed himself to daydream that it was only the two of them, no Ildar, no Chayal, and no Kelandra to chaperone.

After a while, Havyn just gave himself up to the ride. The scenery passed by in a blur of colours, so he wasn't so much aware of his surroundings as he was aware of the heat and bulk of the body behind him. Sometimes Severin's hand slipped from his waist and rested down lower on his hip. Every time it happened, Havyn's groin stirred, and he couldn't help looking down at Severin's well-manicured fingers. It would be so easy for Severin to reach across and caress between his legs, and every time Havyn thought of it, his breath caught and his face heated. Like Ildar had told him, Havyn hadn't indulged in anything that might spill his seed, but he wanted to. Raven how he wanted to!

Havyn didn't know how long they'd travelled before a small town appeared over the horizon by the side of the river. When they got closer, he could make out a wooden sign declaring it to be Aldford. A watermill was the first building, standing right by the river.

"Do you think this is where the uncle lives?" Severin called across to Chayal. "It's the only mill I can see."

"One way to find out," replied Chayal while all of them slowed their horses and dismounted in the market square. They tied the horses to the wooden railing on one side of it. The people in Aldford went on with their daily business and didn't speak about the strangers in their midst. Perhaps the town was used to travellers.

When Havyn dismounted from the horse, his legs gave way beneath him, but Severin was there to hold him up before he fell flat on his face. "Are you all right?"

Havyn nodded. "Thank you, sir," said Havyn, closing his eyes to better appreciate being held in such strong arms, but he knew it couldn't last.

"Severin, that's enough. The lad is fine," said Ildar, almost bodily pulling Havyn out of Severin's embrace. Ildar's voice was better than being dunked in a barrel of cold water, so at least Havyn didn't have to worry about anyone else seeing his body's reaction to being so close to Severin.

Chayal knocked on the door of the water mill, and they waited patiently until it was answered by a matron in a blue dress with a white apron over it. Her hair was covered by a white coif, but a few strands of ebony had escaped their confines and lay in sweaty tendrils on her forehead.

"Yes?" She wiped floury hands on her apron and greeted them in Arcathian.

"Good day, Mistress," said Ildar, bowing low. "We are here to see the miller who is the brother of a fortune-teller in Arcathia. Uncle to Aviel, I believe?"

The woman's face brightened. "That's my husband, Halan. Do come in, he's just gone to the market, but will be back soon." The woman held the door open so they all could come in. Inside was one large room that seemed to serve as kitchen and living space with stairs leading to the upper floors. A scrubbed wooden table was covered with the remains of meal preparation—a rolling pin, flour, flakes of pastry, and fruit. There was a wonderful aroma of bread and fruit pies as they baked in the oven, which was set into the large fireplace.

"Please, have a seat," said the matron, pointing out the chairs and settles around the room. Havyn gingerly sat down on one of the hard wooden seats of the settle, but still winced a little. His thighs and buttocks ached a bit from the horse ride. He hoped they wouldn't have to travel too much further on horseback.

Introductions were made all around, the woman was called Shariel. Soon the bread and the pies were out of the oven and offered to them along with beakers of crisp spring water. After the fare on board the ship, it was a like a feast and they set to it with a will.

"Is Lamil all right?" asked Shariel while she placed second helpings of raspberry pie on everyone's plate.

"She was in perfect health when last we spoke, Mistress Shariel," said Severin. "This is delectable."

The matron blushed at the compliment and bobbed a little curtsey. "Thank you, Lord Severin. We don't often get visitors. Most of my baking ends up at the market."

"Oh, in that case, you must let us repay you for the wonderful fare."

"No, no. Do not think of it, Lord Severin. You are my guests." Shariel glanced out the window. "He's back!" she said with all the excitement of a new bride, her face alight with joy. Havyn wondered if the woman was, in fact, younger than she'd appeared at first.

The wooden door was thrust aside, and a tall man with dark, curly hair and bushy eyebrows entered the space, stooping so he wouldn't hit his head on the lintel. Grey eyes went from his wife to the visitors sitting in his house. He nodded.

"You've come looking for Aviel, I suppose? I thought it would be longer before they sent someone." Halan sat down on one of the wooden kitchen chairs and tugged off his boots with a sigh. "I knew someone would be after them."

"Aviel? You're looking for Aviel?" asked Shariel. "But they left days ago, you've just missed them. What unfortunate luck."

"So Aviel was here? With a girl?" Severin sat up straighter.

"Indeed. He wouldn't reveal the girl's identity, just that there was some trouble with her family and they needed to get away until things calmed down. You're her brother, I suppose?" Halan raised his eyebrows in Severin's direction.

Severin shook his head. "No, I'm her intended bridegroom."

Shariel and Halan exchanged glances.

"What's the matter?" asked Ildar.

"The two of them are already married. They got married in the temple last week."

Chapter Sixteen

Severin could hardly believe his sense of relief at Halan's words. If Ythrin was already married to Aviel, there was no way he could marry her. Dissolutions were almost impossible. But it did beg the question as to what they would do now. What would King Eltan do now that Ythrin had married someone already, never mind a commoner? Would this bring them to the brink of war once again?

"Her uncle still wants her home," Ildar pointed out. "Which way did they go?"

"They went north, but as for their final destination, I do not know," Halan admitted. "Aviel wouldn't confide in me. He was frightened about anyone finding them, but I don't think you mean them harm, do you?"

"No," said Severin. "But it would be best if we did find them. That was our charge." Eltan couldn't expect Severin to keep to his side of the bargain, could he? The man was temperamental at the best of times. What sort of mood would they find him in when they returned with the princess already wed?

"You must rest here and start again in the morning," said Shariel. "It's almost curfew. It will be dark soon." Shariel stood and closed all the window shutters, draping the room in shadows. Halan went around lighting candles and lanterns, both of their hosts seeming nervous.

"A curfew?" asked Chayal. "You have trouble with bandits?"

Shariel turned from one of the windows and shuddered. "No, not bandits."

"Wolven," said Halan, his voice grave as he sat back down.

Chayal and Kelandra made signs to ward off evil, but Havyn looked as mystified as Severin felt.

"What are wolven?" Severin asked. He had never heard the term before.

"They were once men," said Halan. "But no longer. They are now as mindless as animals, and they hunt and kill in packs. They live like wolves, but are far more dangerous. Livestock, children, even smaller adults, none are safe when the wolven are on the prowl. Three men from the town have already been mauled to death. Two more have been bitten and have become wolven themselves. The sickness is in the blood, anyone bitten by a wolven will become one."

"Have you no wizard or priests?" asked Ildar. "Can they not help?"

"How?" asked Halan.

"It is as you say, a sickness, but it is one that can be cured. I can brew a potion that will restore their minds to that of men," said Ildar. "It is a simple matter, but it will take a few days to gather and prepare the ingredients. How many wolven would you say terrorise the town?"

Halan looked at his wife. "Twelve? Thirteen?"

Shariel nodded. "Then you all must stay for as long as you need to. No one has mentioned this potion before. Is it well known in your land?"

"We have never had trouble with wolven," said Ildar.

"Thank you for your hospitality," said Severin. "We accept."

"I'm afraid we don't have any extra beds," said Shariel. "Lord Severin, you must take our room."

"No, Mistress. I cannot oust you from your own beds. We will be quite happy to take the floor."

"Well, we do have pallets, spare blankets, and pillows."

"When you've been travelling for as long as we have, you find you can sleep anywhere," said Severin. "Pallets sound like a luxury, I assure you."

"Halan, why don't you show our guests to the spare room while I start on supper?" asked Shariel. "You can leave your packs here." She pointed to the space underneath the stairs. "There is fresh water so you can freshen up."

"Thank you, you are most kind," said Ildar. Severin shared a glance with Kelandra and surreptitiously nodded in Havyn's direction. Kelandra gave him an almost imperceptible nod.

"Chayal, we have to see to the horses," said Kelandra, grabbing hold of Chayal's arm. "Ildar, I think my mare has a bit of a limp. Can you take a look at her leg and see if it needs a poultice?"

Ildar glanced warily at Havyn, and then at Severin, but Kelandra had taken hold of him too and ushered the two men out the door. Severin could hardly believe it would be so easy to get Havyn alone. Kelandra was such a good friend. When they followed Halan up the stairs, Severin noticed Havyn's delightful blush. His heart beat frantically against his ribs with excitement, and his hands were clammy with sweat.

When they entered the room, Halan came in and out, bringing the pallets and bedding. There was a small table, which had a candle, a sponge, and a basin with a jug of water sitting atop it. The jug was cracked, but Severin didn't mind. As soon as Halan left them alone, he stripped down to his breeches and began to wash his face and chest. Despite being a little thinner after his bout of seasickness, Severin knew he was in good shape and wanted to show off his body to Havyn. Severin lifted his arms to wash under them, stretching his body taut. Havyn gasped behind him. Severin smiled to himself and turned around, his face impassive once more.

"Havyn, don't you need a wash too?" asked Severin, holding out the sponge, the water dripping with small 'plops' onto the wooden floor.

Havyn visibly swallowed as he took the offered sponge and began to wash his face without removing any of his clothes.

"Shirt off," said Severin. "You're probably so sticky after the horse ride. The water's wonderfully refreshing."

Severin wondered if Havyn would make any objection, but considering they would both be naked to the waist, perhaps Havyn didn't mind because he set the sponge down on the table while he removed his tunic and undershirt. Severin let his gaze travel from Havyn's head to the waistband of his leggings. He felt like whistling in appreciation.

"Your chest is so smooth," said Severin, lifting the sponge and beginning to wash Havyn's chest without asking. Havyn didn't protest, and Severin wondered if it was because the boy was used to doing what he was told without thought for his own needs or desires. Perhaps he didn't really want this? Didn't really want Severin?

Havyn closed his eyes and swayed slightly, his hands fisted at his sides.

"Ildar said it's because of the Aldari. They are smooth too, no hair except for their heads and eyebrows."

"Really?" Severin glanced down at Havyn's groin, noticing the growing bulge there. He smiled again. It seemed that despite Ildar's anti-sex lessons, Havyn was still capable of desire. What would happen if he reached out and kissed Havyn? Would Havyn push him away? Severin's mouth watered at the thought of kissing those delectable lips. He set the sponge down and dipped his hands in the water before returning to Havyn's chest and rubbing the water all over his neck and chest again. Havyn moaned and swayed against him.

Havyn's nipples stood up in little points, but Severin didn't know if it was because of the chill of the water or because he was enjoying the caresses. Severin's own nipples peaked in sympathy. He caressed the smooth planes of Havyn's chest. The blood pounded in his ears and pooled in his groin. Halan had finished bringing all the pallets and they wouldn't be disturbed until the others returned, but Severin went to the door and latched it just in case.

Havyn's eyes flew open at the noise. "Master Severin?"

"When we're alone you may call me Severin," he replied, turning back to Havyn, it was quite an uncomfortable walk. "I'm not a king with you, Havyn. I'm just a man."

"I—" Havyn began, but Severin stopped him by pressing a forefinger to Havyn's lips.

"Sssh. No words. Not now. I just want you to feel."

Severin had kissed his fair share of girls at all of the balls his parents had hosted at the palace, but until now, he had never dared to contemplate kissing a man. Havyn looked up at him with something akin to awe, his eyes bright, and Severin relished it. "You know I can't lie to you," whispered Severin. "I want you, Havyn. Do you understand?" Havyn was a little bit younger than him, and Severin wondered if perhaps Havyn hadn't yet understood what two men could do together.

Havyn nodded, his eyes fluttering closed, his mouth hanging half-open. Severin took that as an invitation, and he leaned closer to Havyn, so close their chests were almost touching. He cupped Havyn's face in his hands and pressed his lips softly against Havyn's. His eyes closed at the sensation while the two of them stood there stealing the breath from each other. Severin knew he wanted a lot more than kisses, but he didn't want to scare Havyn away with too much too soon, despite his own desire. Severin let his hands wander down Havyn's back, trailing softly over his skin. He held back the moans that wanted to fly free from his throat.

Severin only pulled away from the kiss when his need for air became too great. Havyn stared at him with wide eyes, his fingers trailing along his lips, as if he couldn't quite believe it had happened. "You kissed me," Havyn said with a sigh.

"I'd like to do it again if you will permit it," said Severin. "I only want what you are willing to give me."

"Everything," breathed Havyn. "But Lord Ildar said I mustn't."

"What Ildar doesn't know won't hurt him," said Severin. "I won't take your virtue, Havyn. There are other ways we can take pleasure with each other."

"But he said I mustn't spill my seed or I will lose my powers," Havyn said, flushing scarlet.

"Do you sometimes have dreams that make you sticky?" asked Severin, unable to get the image of a gasping Havyn, lost in pleasure, out of his head.

"Yes."

"Could you still use your powers afterward?"

Havyn cocked his head to one side as if remembering something. He nodded. "Yes. Does that mean Ildar is wrong?"

"Some younger wizards believe that wizarding power has got nothing at all to do with what a wizard does with his seed. They even get married and have families."

"Really? Ildar never mentioned that." Havyn dried himself off, and much to Severin's chagrin, covered up that lovely, smooth chest. Severin imagined he could still feel the satiny flesh under his fingertips and they tingled with the memory.

"His ideas are considered quite old fashioned now, but he is a powerful wizard so perhaps for him, the sacrifice of giving up a family was worth it. But yes there are indeed wizards in Arcathia now with families or lovers."

"Oh."

"Place your pallet next to mine tonight," said Severin when he heard footsteps coming up the stairs. "Please." Severin unlatched the door, not wanting anyone to wonder why it had been locked in the first place. He turned back to Havyn. "Please."

Havyn nodded and turned away just as the door was flung open. Ildar stood there panting like one of their horses.

"Anyone would think that girl had never ridden a horse before. There was nothing wrong with the beast at all. Nothing!"

Ildar huffed and puffed, staring at the bowl of water. "I suppose it would be a bit rude to ask our hosts for hot water, would it not?"

"It would indeed," said Severin. "They have put themselves out enough on our account."

"I can heat it for you, Master Ildar," said Havyn, placing his hands on the bowl and mumbling some words under his breath. Steam rose from the bowl, making both Ildar and Severin gape in surprise.

"Havyn, I haven't taught you that spell. How did you know what to do?"

Havyn shrugged. "It just seemed natural."

"Excellent. You can both go back downstairs now and leave an old man to his washing."

"You're not old, Ildar." Severin chuckled. "You'll end up burying us all."

"I hope not, lad," said Ildar, making a sign to ward off bad luck. "Off with you now. I'll be down for supper."

Severin grinned at Havyn, they had to stifle their mirth while heading back downstairs. Ildar never missed a meal if he could help it.

Chapter Seventeen

Havyn could barely eat the wonderful meal Shariel had prepared for them. Although the food was plain compared to what was served at the palace, it was a lot better than the food on board the ship had been, and there was plenty of it. Chicken so tender that it almost fell off the bone before a knife went anywhere near it and vegetables cooked crisp, but tasty. Again, they were all offered water to drink rather than alcohol, but after so much wine and ale aboard the ship, no one seemed to mind the water.

The reason for Havyn's lack of appetite tonight wasn't illness like it had been before, but rather nervousness. What did Severin plan on doing with the others right there in the room with them? "Mistress Shariel, let me help you with the jug," said Severin, standing up from his place at the table. Kelandra and Chayal glanced at Severin, and then at each other. It wasn't often Severin offered to help, especially in a role more suited to a servant. Havyn, in turn, felt slightly guilty. Perhaps he should have offered to help their hostess, too? It was too late now anyway. Severin already had the jug filled and was pouring water into Ildar, Chayal, and Kelandra's wooden beakers.

Just as he was about to fill Havyn's beaker, Severin lost control of the jug and spilled the remainder on the floor

"So sorry," said Severin with a sheepish grin in Shariel's direction.

"Not to worry. We have more in the pantry," said Shariel. "Halan, can you go and fetch the other jug?"

Halan kissed her on the cheek before heading off to the pantry. Ildar, Chayal, and Kelandra swigged down their water while Havyn and Severin waited for the fresh jug from Halan. Havyn wondered if Severin was nervous too. Was that why he'd spilled the water when he reached Havyn? He tried to catch Severin's eye, but the young king seemed to avoid looking at him. Perhaps Severin already regretted what had happened between them. Havyn picked at the rest of his meal, but found his appetite had fled. He pushed the food around on his plate, hoping no one noticed how little he was eating.

Halan returned and handed a jug to Shariel. "I think I'll pour this time, Lord Severin," she smiled at him while she filled their beakers. Opposite them, Ildar yawned and placed a hand over his mouth.

"Oh dear. The journey has caught up with me. I'm afraid I shall retire if that's all right?"

"Of course, Master Ildar," said Shariel. "Rest is good for the soul."

A few moments later, Kelandra and Chayal excused themselves also, both yawning profusely. Although dark, it wasn't particularly late, and Havyn wondered what had suddenly made their companions so tired. Halan and Severin entered into a discussion on what made the best wood for a bow, something Havyn had no knowledge of and wasn't that interested in. He had never hunted nor had he been trained with any weapons, so he helped Shariel wash and dry the dishes while the two men were deep in conversation.

"Thank you for your help, Havyn," said Shariel once the last plate was washed and put away in the rack on the wall.

"You're welcome."

"I think it's time we went to bed, too," said Severin. "Thank you again for your hospitality."

"It was our pleasure," said Shariel, smiling at both of them. "Halan, give the boys a candle to light their way."

Halan fetched a candle from a box on the floor, and set it into a pewter holder before lighting it and handing it to Severin. "Goodnight, Mistress Shariel, Master Halan," said Severin. Havyn, too, bade them goodnight, and then followed Severin back upstairs to the bedroom they all shared. The candle flame flickered wildly as they made their way upstairs.

Severin pushed the door open, and peeked inside. He then turned back to Havyn. "They're all asleep."

Even from the hallway, Havyn could hear Ildar's snores. They tiptoed into the room, careful not to disturb the others. "Why were they all so tired?" Havyn whispered. "I don't feel that tired at all."

Severin grinned at him. Havyn caught a flash of white teeth from the light of the candle. "I put a sleeping draught in their water. That's why I didn't want you to drink that one. I wanted you wide awake tonight."

Havyn swallowed. His whole body heated as if he'd suddenly been plunged into a fire. "You still—you still want..."

"Oh, my dearest Havyn. Yes, I still want you. How could I not?" Severin reached out and caressed Havyn's left cheek. In his other hand, the candle wavered and wax dripped onto the floor. "Hold on a moment."

Severin set the candle down on the small table, but didn't put it out, so they could still see the position of the others. There were two empty pallets, one on the other side of Chayal and one on the other side of Ildar. Havyn knew that Ildar would expect him to sleep next to him, but between Severin and Havyn, they managed to move both pallets, fitting them together on the floor, lying sideways by the others' feet.

Havyn's blood pounded in his ears as they disrobed down to their underlinens. The muted candlelight caressed their skin and made Severin's hair almost invisible. Severin's gaze never left his as he lay down on one of the pallets and patted the one next to him to indicate that Havyn should lie down too.

"We'll have to be quiet," Severin whispered. "We don't want to wake them."

Havyn nodded. He didn't want Ildar to wake and discover what they were doing. He didn't think Kelandra or Chayal would mind, but Havyn knew Ildar wouldn't approve. Perhaps Ildar might even refuse to train him any longer. What would he do then?

Severin scooted over and opened his arms so that he could wrap Havyn in them. Havyn gasped when they touched chest to chest. Severin had sparse hair there that tickled Havyn's own smooth chest.

"You're so beautiful, Havyn," Severin whispered, his breath hot in Havyn's ear. Havyn stifled a groan as he tried to angle his body away from Severin's. He was hard and aching, and he didn't want Severin to know, but Severin didn't let him go anywhere. Severin grabbed hold of Havyn's waist and tugged Havyn toward him.

"May I kiss you some more?" Severin asked softly.

Havyn nodded, not trusting himself to speak. He was all too aware of the others in the room, and the heat of Severin's body next to him. His lower belly tingled with excitement as he closed his eyes and felt the first soft press of Severin's lips on his. It was wonderful to be kissed. The sensations nearly swept him away. The kiss started out soft, but soon it became more frantic. Severin pulled him close until they were no longer just kissing; they were devouring each other's souls through their mouths.

Havyn's staff throbbed against Severin's leg, and he could feel an echoing hardness against his own. Rocking wildly together, they kissed and kissed. When Severin pushed his tongue into Havyn's mouth and pressed it against his own, Havyn felt a jolt of desire so strong he was sure if he hadn't been lying down, he would have fallen. Severin moved, tumbling Havyn beneath him, and then rutting against him, still with those breath-stealing kisses.

Severin pulled his mouth away from Havyn's, and then began to lick and suck his neck, his lower body pressing hard against Havyn. Havyn arched up from the pallet, his legs instinctively going around Severin's waist while he rocked against him.

"Havyn!" Severin gasped, grabbing hold of his wrists and pinning them to the pallet, his movements suddenly speeding up. "Ohhh!"Severin stiffened above him, his thrusting erratic. Dampness seeped through Havyn's underlinens when Severin reached his crisis. The wet heat, the weight of the man on top of him, it was all too much for him, too. Havyn's hips bucked as his climax soared through him. He bit his lip to stop himself from crying out when his seed spilled from him in ecstatic pulses that made the inside of his underlinens a sticky, damp mess.

They panted harshly, and Havyn glanced over at the others. They were all still fast asleep, Ildar snoring away, oblivious to anything the two of them might have been up to. Severin kissed him deeply, and then rolled off him, holding his arms out again. Havyn took the comfort offered and snuggled up, leaning his head on Severin's chest. Severin caressed his hair and kissed the top of his head, making him want to purr like a kitten. He felt safe in his lover's arms. Loved. He could sense it.

"Do you know any cleaning spells?" Severin asked, waving at their groins.

Havyn nodded. A few moments later, both their clothes and they were dry once again.

"You feel guilty about deceiving Ildar, don't you?" asked Severin.

"He's always been so nice to me. I don't want to hurt him."

"I doubt us being together would hurt him," replied Severin. "Do you realise what you just did?"

"No, what?"

"You did magic after you'd spilled your seed."

"Oh." Despite the knowledge that Ildar may have been wrong about a wizard losing his power if he spilled his seed, the guilt in his chest didn't ease.

* * * *

"Ah. Here we are," said Ildar, bending down and examining a silvery leaf. "Cotton lavender. Just what we need to finish off the potion."

The others were still back at the mill, but Ildar had insisted that Havyn accompany him in his search for ingredients for the potion as part of his studies. They had already discovered lots of the plants they needed. Havyn had them in the basket they had borrowed from Shariel.

"Are there really men who turn into wolves, Master Ildar?" Havyn asked, bending down to the wizard's level.

Ildar cut the stems and added them to Havyn's basket. "Dear me, no. What put that idea into your head? No, wolven don't turn into wolves. It's just a name. Those poor men have lost their minds, but they don't grow fur and teeth. It's a mental disorder, but some people can be a little superstitious and stories get out of proportion."

"Oh." Havyn stood and stretched, scanning the horizon, but all he could see was the town in the distance and the mill wheel turning by the river.

"Havyn, lad, is everything all right? You don't seem yourself this morning."

"I'm fine. Perhaps just a bit tired." A flash of heat went through Havyn's body as he remembered the reason for his tiredness. A memory of a strong body pressed against his flew through his mind, and he knew he was blushing again. He turned away so Ildar wouldn't see it and wonder. Technically, it wasn't a lie. Havyn was tired, and long after Severin had fallen into a sated sleep, he had lain awake, tendrils of guilt coiling in his gut as he thought of how disappointed Ildar would be in him if he ever found out what they'd done.

When Ildar pressed a hand on Havyn's shoulder, he almost jumped out of his skin.

"My, you are skittish today. I didn't mean to startle you. I've got everything we need now. We just need to brew it. We can see if Mistress Shariel can let us have a loan of one of her saucepans. It'll take a few days to complete."

Ildar patted Havyn on the shoulder and turned him around to face him. He tilted Havyn's chin up. "If anything is bothering you, you know you can talk to me, all right? I know everything must be a bit strange and new for you, but I promise I won't bite."

"Thank you, Master Ildar. But I'm fine. Really."

"If you're sure?"

Havyn nodded, and the two of them made their way back to the mill.

Chapter Eighteen

Chayal and Kelandra had gone off somewhere in the town to gather more supplies for the rest of their journey, leaving Ildar and Havyn brewing in Shariel's kitchen. Severin sat on a stool watching them. Shariel and Halan were away working at the mill already this morning. There had been plenty of farmers with their grain ready to be milled. Severin had never put much thought into where his food came from before. The palace had an army of cooks and there was always something to eat whenever it was wanted. Being on the road made him appreciate how much effort actually went into it.

Ildar had two large black pots on the table, he stirred one while Havyn chopped up various plants and put them into the other. Havyn's hands flew through the preparation as if he'd done this many times before. During his tutelage, Ildar had never let Severin anywhere near his precious plants and herbs. Severin's cutting had been too coarse, and his hands clumsy so he never learned to brew anything, not even a simple poultice. He stared at Havyn's hands, remembering those hands on him last night. The young wizard had barely spoken to him or looked at him this morning. Severin wondered if he had scared him by going too fast. Havyn had just been so tempting that it had been impossible to hold back. It had been nothing like the times he'd kissed the girls his parents had thrust in front of him, keen to get him married as soon as possible. He wondered if his mother knew of his father's death yet. How would she take the news?

The sun streaming through the open shutters fell on Havyn's hair like a halo, and it was all too easy to imagine the young man as someone otherworldly. His dark curls glinted with chestnut highlights in the sunlight, and his eyes seemed to glow with some inner fire that made Severin's chest ache. He wondered if Havyn had inadvertently cast a lust spell on him because Severin had never felt such heat as there had been with Havyn last night. Severin's lips were swollen and sore this morning after so much kissing the previous night. It had been wonderful, but Severin wished Havyn would look at him or at least acknowledge him to let him know that he had enjoyed it too.

Severin continued to stare at Havyn, not having anything else to do. The others were getting supplies and Ildar didn't want Severin's help. It seemed he was a bit of a third leg, and tried not to sulk about feeling so useless. He'd offered to help out at the mill, but Halan wouldn't hear of it, protesting that he was a guest and should rest.

He'd done nothing but rest, and he was itching for some activity. When Havyn glanced up, and their eyes caught for a brief moment, Severin knew that it wasn't just any activity he wanted. He wanted to get Havyn alone again, pin him beneath him, and kiss him senseless. His loins ached with the wanting of it. Severin crossed his legs, willing his passion down. There was nothing to be done about it at the moment. Maybe not for a few days either. He couldn't keep slipping sleeping draughts to their companions, much as he might wish to.

Havyn blushed, and then looked down again. He had a habit of biting his lower lip when he was nervous, and he was doing it now. The flush to Havyn's normally pale cheeks, the reddened lips, the lowered eyes, and the memories of their time last night, none of it was helping ease Severin's frustrations. He couldn't spend a moment longer in the kitchen with Havyn or he'd go mad.

"I'm going for a walk," he announced, striding from the table.

"Don't get lost," warned Ildar.

"I won't go far," said Severin. There was a wood on the edge of the town. He could at least find some privacy for a while, and if things didn't calm down, he could always take matters into his own hands. As he left the house, he almost ran to the woods, wanting to get some space as soon as possible. Townsfolk greeted him when he passed, but he was barely aware of them, still lost in a world of his own.

By the time he reached the shade of the trees, he was already sweating. He was so hot, he was sure he could heat up Ildar's potion without the need for a fire. Severin walked deeper into the woods until he came to a glade with a small pool. There was a small waterfall cascading down a rocky wall behind it. The spray was delightfully cool on his heated face. Severin sat down by the edge of the pool to tug off his boots and stockings. He hissed in pleasure when he dipped his feet. The water was so refreshing on his skin.

Severin wondered if come autumn, Ythrin and Aviel would be found. The cooler weather of the changing seasons couldn't come soon enough. As a child, illness had left him with circulation problems and summer made him sweat, but winter made him freeze, more so than most people. Autumn was just perfect, so he hoped that by that time, he was free do as he pleased.

There was no one else around, and Severin decided he could risk bathing in the pool. The coolness of the water was too inviting to pass up. It might help cool his ardour, too. Severin stood up to strip off his shirt, breeches, and underlinens. He stood on tiptoes, arching his body toward the heavens, his arms outstretched as the sun beamed down on his skin. He didn't know how long he stood there, naked as the day he was born with his manhood jutting out and pointing straight at the water.

When he stepped into the pool, he gasped at the sudden drop in temperature as it reached his waist. It did indeed cool his ardour. There was no way he could stay hard in water so cold. He swam over to the waterfall and stood under it, the cool liquid sluicing over his body and bubbling in the pool once more. The rock behind his back was warm, obviously the sun shone on this part of the pool more than where he had first entered.

Severin leaned back against the wall and saw the world through the curtain of falling water now that he was positioned behind it. Already the sun was warming him again, and Severin's thoughts turned once more to Havyn. Had Havyn regretted what they'd done so soon? Severin trailed a hand along his chest, pinching his nipple as he went. There was no one else about for the moment, but he wished he was able to do one of Ildar's notice-me-not spells just to make sure. It would have been rather embarrassing to be caught pleasuring himself, but Severin knew his desire would return as soon as he saw Havyn unless he did something now.

His shaft already rose from its nest of fair curls. The waterfall would hide him if anyone happened to come by, at least he would look a bit blurred, and it wouldn't be so obvious what he was doing. He rested against the rocky wall behind him, parts of it jutted out and poked him, but it was a lot easier to have something to lean against, for Severin was sure his legs wouldn't be able to support him much longer.

From as far back as he could remember, Severin had enjoyed pleasuring himself. It wasn't a practice frowned upon in Arcathia, in fact, it was encouraged in order to keep people virgins until their initiation. Sometimes, he was in the mood to tease himself, letting the sensations build and build until he could no longer contain it. Other times, it was just something he did to ease himself in order to sleep and he was done quickly.

Today, although he was in the mood for teasing himself, he didn't want to get caught, so he knew he would have to be quicker than he would have liked. He gripped his shaft in his hand and stroked himself hard, thrusting his hips forward as he sought the peak. Memories and fantasies of Havyn collided until Severin wasn't even sure that it was his own hand. It was Havyn's hand stroking him, fondling the sac between his legs as Severin gasped and bucked, spilling his seed into the water. His legs trembled as he panted for breath. The world started coming back into focus again.

Severin swam a few more laps of the pool before getting out and letting the sun dry his skin. He dozed for a while, and when he opened his eyes, he thought he saw Havyn standing over him. All he could see was dark hair and violet eyes.

"Havyn?" Severin gasped, sitting up and gathering his clothes to him in some sort of modest gesture when he realised it wasn't Havyn at all, but a woman. Her long dark hair was like a curtain down her back and it wasn't as curly as Havyn's at all. Her eyes were like Havyn's though, and Severin couldn't help staring at her. She was wearing a long white robe like the priestesses wore, but unlike them, this one's robe was soaking wet and clinging to her curves like a second skin.

"You have summoned me, mortal. What do you seek?"

"I don't understand."

"I am the guardian of this pool. You have made an offering, and now you are entitled to a boon."

"Who are you?" asked Severin, clutching his clothes tighter to his chest.

The woman didn't smile. In fact, she didn't seem to have very many emotions on her face at all.

"I am one of the Guardians. One of the Chosen."

"The Chosen? You're Aldari? I thought Aldari didn't walk in the world anymore?"

"They do not. Not by choice."

"Then why are you here?"

"You have summoned me. It is an old pact between our races. When a mortal makes an offering at certain guarded places, we are obliged to answer their call and give them a boon."

"But I didn't summon you!" protested Severin. "I haven't offered you anything."

"You spilled your seed in the pool. You made an offering. Now, what is your boon?"

"Er, I can't think of anything."

"You must or I will be forced to remain here until you do."

"Oh, I can't let that happen," said Severin, wracking his brain for something. "We are seeking Princess Ythrin and her husband, Aviel. Can you tell me where they are?"

"I am sorry, that is a boon I cannot grant."

"Why not?"

"They are under another Guardian's protection, I cannot see them."

"Oh." Severin couldn't think of anything else he wanted to know.

"Do you have a sweetheart? Perhaps you wish someone to fall in love with you?"

Severin's mind immediately went to Havyn, and tempting though it was, he knew he didn't want Havyn to fall in love with him because of some sort of magic. "No. Can you tell me if someone is in love with me though?"

"I can. What is their name?"

"Havyn."

The woman closed her eyes, and for a brief moment, she smiled. "Havyn. A beautiful man. His heart is filled with love for you. But sadness and guilt too. He does not like deception. Until he met you he had never lied, never uttered a deceitful word. I see that he is confused, but determined. He wants to make you happy and...Ildar, is it? He loves you, but your love will not be enough. Havyn needs commitment and stability. A family. I sense great sadness for both of you."

The woman opened her eyes. "Your boon has been granted."

She disappeared. "Wait!" Severin called to the empty air, but she was gone long before Severin could ask her anything else.

Chapter Nineteen

Four days later, Ildar's potion had been distributed to the families of the townsfolk who had become infected, and later that evening, the people had thanked Ildar in broken Arcathian for returning their loved ones to sanity once again. The townsfolk showed their gratitude with many gifts and so much food they couldn't possibly accommodate it all. Their last night in Aldford, a feast in their honour was held in the town square.

There was music and dancing, and even Ildar got up to dance with one of the matrons when she offered him her hand. Chayal and Kelandra looked at each other, and then got up to dance with each other, too, leaving Havyn and Severin alone on one of the wooden benches that had been set up around the square. The moon was a quarter full and Havyn stared at it rather than at Severin. He wanted to dance with Severin, but knew that it wasn't a possibility, not if they wanted to keep their feelings secret from Ildar.

"Havyn? Have I done something wrong?" Severin asked, scooting closer to him. "Did I take things too far?"

Havyn turned, but he didn't need to see Severin's face to know how the other man was feeling. He could sense Severin's sadness already. "No. It's not that. I loved being with you, and I want to be with you again, but I'm worried about Ildar finding out."

"We'll just have to be more careful," said Severin. "I thought you were upset about what we'd done."

Havyn smiled and blushed. "No. Never. I was just nervous. I've never done anything like that before."

"Me neither," Severin admitted.

Before Havyn could reply, Kelandra and Chayal returned from their dance, giggling and stumbling. Havyn suspected that they'd had a bit too much of the dandelion wine. "A dance, Havyn?" asked Kelandra, holding out her hand. Havyn looked at Severin, who nodded. Havyn took the bodyguard's hand and followed her onto the makeshift dance floor. Havyn had never danced before, but most people just seemed to be jumping around to the energetic music. It wasn't a dance where he needed to put his arms around her to guide her across the floor.

Kelandra sidled close to him. "He's watching you," she said.

"Who? Ildar?"

Kelandra laughed. "No, Severin, silly. He can't take his eyes off you."

Havyn's whole body heated at that thought. It felt good to be so desired, but he was worried, too. "Do you think Ildar has noticed?"

"Noticed what? That the two of you have been staring at each other like moonstruck calves for the past few days?"

"Are we that obvious?" Havyn asked, appalled that they'd given themselves away.

"Not to Ildar," said Kelandra, nodding in the wizard's direction. Ildar smiled jovially while he danced with one of the townswomen. "Ildar is not on the same plane as the rest of us. His mind is usually on higher things than love and lust."

"You won't tell him?"

"Of course not. I think it's wonderful that you and Severin have found each other. I knew Severin would never be happy married to a woman. He has never shown them the slightest bit of interest. Now that Ythrin is already married, perhaps Severin will be free to live his own life. I don't know what King Eltan is going to say about the matter though."

"Do you think we'll find the princess and her husband?"

"Chayal's a good tracker. If we follow the road north like Halan said, I think we can catch up with them."

Havyn nodded, wondering if it would be that easy.

* * * *

They'd been on the road north for at least a week, but Havyn was finding it difficult to keep track of the days. Each day he rode with Severin had been bittersweet because his body remembered Severin's soft touches in the dark and responded accordingly when they were so close to each other for hours at a time. But with Ildar and the others so close by, there was nothing to be done, and he had to try to think of the most vile things to quench his desire. He knew Severin was having the same problem—the evidence was pressing against his back while they rode.

It was starting to get dark, and Havyn knew they would be stopping to camp soon. He leaned back against Severin and angled his head around. "Tonight?" he whispered, knowing he couldn't bear the tension much longer. Severin nodded against his head just as Chayal called a halt and they began to set up camp.

"Kelandra, you and Havyn can gather some firewood," said Ildar, unpacking his bedroll and smoothing it out, clucking with disappointment. The wizard hated camping. "It gets cold at night here, don't you find? We'll need a fire for the cooking."

"I'll help," said Severin. "Or do you need me to help with the horses, Chayal?"

"No, Lord Severin. I can manage," Chayal said with a wink. Havyn wondered how many other people knew about his and Severin's feelings for each other. The three of them made their way further into the woods by the side of the road in order to find some loose branches.

"Oh, look," Kelandra said rather obviously pointing to the distance. "I think I'll search over there, you two will be fine on your own, won't you?"

They grinned and nodded. When Kelandra was out of sight, Severin wasted no time in pushing Havyn up against the trunk of a tree. They were so close their faces were almost touching. In the fading light, Severin looked at him with something akin to awe, and he revelled in it. For so long he'd been powerless, but when Severin looked at him like that, he had power. Havyn tilted his head up and closed his eyes, unable to bear such intense scrutiny any longer. Havyn's heart beat an erratic rhythm against his ribcage as he waited for the kiss. He wanted to yank open his chest and hand Severin his still beating heart to do with what he would.

The wait seemed to last an eternity. He was aware of the rough bark against his back, the smell of damp earth and leaves in his nostrils, the songs of the birds coming home to roost for the night, the rustle of leaves in the breeze, and the weight of Severin pressed against him. Just as he took a deep breath, it happened. Severin's lips pressed down hard against his own. For so long, Havyn had been dreaming of their next kiss, but nothing could have prepared him for the reality of it. For the wet heat of Severin's lips upon his as they crushed their mouths' together, with barely a breadth of air between them. It was like Severin knew what Havyn wanted. Severin wasn't just kissing him, he was claiming him, setting Havyn aflame, and by the Raven if he didn't want to stand here and let himself be consumed until there was nothing left of him but ashes.

Havyn was getting light headed, but he didn't want to stop. Severin moaned and Havyn felt the vibrations deep in the back of his own throat. When Severin's tongue pushed through his lips, Havyn groaned, forgetting everything but the two of them. He tugged the young king toward him, Severin's body nestling between his legs. He wanted more of these sensations that fluttered around his belly like butterflies too scared to land on an exotic flower. He chased them, but they were as elusive as water trickling through his fingers.

Havyn grabbed hold of Severin's neck and tried to get as close as possible without sharing the same skin. Severin shifted, and his body fell heavily against Havyn's, moulding him to the tree. Havyn could feel the evidence of Severin's desire pressing against him, and he moaned again. The thought that he had done this, he had made the man want him, made his own arousal spike, and he kissed Severin hungrily, almost violently.

Severin pulled back, gasping for air before raining kisses all along Havyn's neck and jaw. Havyn arched his neck back against the trunk of the tree. Severin rewarded him when he licked him, nipping at the sensitive skin like a cat lapping at a bowl of cream. Havyn mewled. "Please. Oh, please!" Havyn begged.

Severin somehow managed to get a hand between them and cupped Havyn's shaft through his breeches, making his knees weak. It didn't take long, Havyn knew he was too far gone in pleasure, and all too soon it happened, he was spilling himself in his breeches. He reached out for the bulge in Severin's breeches, and soon, Severin spilled too.

"Ildar's coming," Kelandra whispered urgently when she reached them at a run. Havyn quickly cast the cleaning spell over both of them, and despite his wobbly legs, they began to gather up bundles of firewood as the wizard approached.

"Excellent. I was just gathering some more wild mushrooms. We can add them to the stew. You all look a bit flushed. I hope you're not coming down with anything."

* * * *

The next morning, Havyn felt much better about riding with Severin. He was still sated from their loving the night before. Now it was possible not to get so worked up, and he could just let himself enjoy being held in Severin's arms while they rode along the northern road.

"Here," cried Chayal, holding up his hand so they all stopped behind him. The horses whinnied and stamped their hooves impatiently. Ildar and Kelandra dismounted and looked at the burnt patch of ground by the side of the road. "A campfire. Quite recent, too. I think they've been through here."

Severin dismounted, too, leaving Havyn the only one seated on a horse. He watched while the others circled around the camp, trying to discover any more clues about where its occupants might have gone next. Suddenly, Havyn cried out in shock when he was pulled from the horse. The others turned, three of them reaching for their swords.

A metal blade pressed against Havyn's throat. He didn't dare move.

"None of you come any closer or he's dead!" a male voice snarled. Havyn couldn't see his attacker, but he could guess at his identity.

"Aviel?" he ventured.

"How do you know my name?" the man demanded, pressing the blade even deeper into Havyn's flesh. It stung a bit, but the pain was manageable. Havyn wasn't worried about pain. Yet, the threat terrified him. He could almost see his lifeless body on the forest floor, a river of crimson leaking from his throat.

"We were looking for you," said Ildar, holding his palms out to show that he had no weapons. "You and the princess."

"We're not going back! Do you think we're fools? Her uncle will murder us. We know the laws in Oscia," sneered Aviel.

"Those laws have been repealed," said Severin. "King Eltan signed them before we left. Marriage is now legal again, you can return in safety."

"Safety? This is some trick! I'm not going anywhere with you and neither is Ythrin. They were trying to marry her off to some prince from Arcathia. She loves me." There was desperation in the man's voice.

"We know that, Aviel," said Ildar calmly. "Now that you are married, she cannot be married to anyone else. There is nothing to fear if you return to Oscia."

"Do you think her uncle will be pleased that she married a commoner? A peasant?"

"Love knows no boundaries of class," said Ildar. "The king will come around, especially if Ythrin is to give him an heir. That was the reason he wanted her married in the first place."

Aviel's hand shook as he held the knife, but he didn't relinquish it.

"Aviel, let them speak," came another voice, a female one that reminded Havyn of bells ringing. He heard soft footfalls on the leafy ground, and then she was there. Wavy black hair cascaded loosely around her shoulders. Her violet eyes were the match to Havyn's own. He stared, gape-mouthed at her. "I dreamed you would come," said Ythrin, reaching out and plucking the knife from Aviel's hand. "The prince from Arcathia."

"I'm not the prince," said Havyn. "Severin was the prince."

Ythrin glanced across at Severin and shook her head. "I wasn't dreaming of the Prince of Arcathia. I was dreaming of the prince *from* Arcathia. That is you, Havyn. You are my cousin."

"Your cousin? But then that would mean..."

"Yes. King Eltan is your father."

Chapter Twenty

H avyn!" Severin called when he saw the young man sway and stumble toward the ground. Severin rushed to his side and caught him before he fell. Everyone else in the clearing looked astounded at the news, but Ythrin remained calmly impassive to the shock she'd just hit Havyn with. Havyn was a prince? Eltan's son? But hadn't Eltan's son died? At least, that was what Severin had been told over the years.

"Some water?" Severin asked of no one in particular as he gently lowered Havyn to the ground. Havyn groaned, but he didn't come around. Kelandra thrust a water skin into Severin's hand. Severin removed the stopper with his teeth before angling Havyn's head up, resting it on one arm and pressing the mouth of the container against his lips.

When Severin pressed the water to Havyn's lips, the young wizard coughed and spluttered, most of the liquid dribbling down his chin. His eyes fluttered open, his violet gaze seeking out Severin. There was no need to be a wizard to see the alarm in Havyn's eyes. The others crowded around them, and as much as Severin wanted to be the one to offer Havyn some comfort, he knew he couldn't. Not with Ildar only a few yards away from them. In the pretence of trying to struggle to his feet, Severin squeezed Havyn's arm. Havyn nodded almost imperceptibly as though to let him know he understood. Havyn seemed grateful for even that scrap of comfort, something done almost unthinkingly.

When Severin rose, it brought home to him even more how difficult Havyn's life as a slave must have been, even more so than the scars that covered Havyn's torso. How must it have felt to know that there would be no gentle touches or caresses, but only the smack of a fist or the kick of a boot? To live each day in fear rather than contentment? To live in despair rather than hope? And now, to discover that he had been a prince all along and should never have had to suffer such degradation at all.

Ildar helped Havyn up and settled him against a tree before the wizard turned to the princess. "Princess Ythrin, forgive me, but how do you know Havyn is your cousin? Everyone was under the impression that both of Eltan's children died along with their mother in childbirth."

"My mother told me," replied Ythrin, looking curiously at Havyn. The young man's colour was returning, but he didn't seem back to himself quite yet. Severin ached to hold him and tell him that everything was going to be all right, even if it wasn't.

"Your mother? But isn't your mother dead too?"

"Yes. I'm not going mad. She speaks to me in my dreams, and she has told me what really happened the night my aunt Xiana died."

"Your aunt died in complications during childbirth, did she not?" continued Ildar, wiping sweat from his brow. His face was turning an alarming shade of purple and he clutched hard at his chest, breathing heavily.

"Master Ildar!" Havyn cried, jumping to his feet and helping the wizard down to the ground and making him lean back against the tree Havyn had so recently been resting against.

"I'm fine, lad. I just need a moment's rest, that's all."

Severin wasn't convinced of that, and when Havyn glanced worriedly over his shoulder, Severin knew he wasn't convinced of Ildar's perfect health either.

Everyone else sat down around him, and Severin felt as if they were all Ildar's students, waiting to hear what their tutor had to say, but he knew it was Ythrin's words everyone waited on. "Please go on, your highness," said Ildar, puffing like he'd just finished a race. Havyn sat next to him, holding Ildar's hand. "Your aunt didn't die in childbirth, then?"

"She died that night, but not in childbirth. My mother had gone to attend her along with one of the midwives from the castle. The girl was born first, my uncle didn't know Xiana was carrying twins, and neither did anyone else. Oscian midwifery is not as advanced as that in Arcathia. There was no way of telling until the children were born. Once the girl was born, Eltan rejected her."

"Rejected her? What does that mean?" asked Havyn.

"It is a custom in Oscia that children who are rejected by their fathers are taken away and left."

"Left where?"

"In the woods or on the mountains. They usually do not survive the night, either dying from exposure or from animal attacks."

"Left to die? An innocent child?" asked Havyn.

"It is the Oscian way."

"Well, it's not my way," Havyn retorted hotly.

"You're Oscian," said Ythrin.

"*No!* I refuse to believe it."

"Refusing to believe it will not make it any less so," Ythrin pointed out. "You are Oscian, Havyn, and King Eltan is your father."

"I want nothing to do with that murderer," ranted Havyn. "He is nothing to me. Nothing!"

"Well, he is a murderer," said Ythrin calmly. "You can reject him as much as he rejected your sister."

"Selling me into slavery? Was that Eltan's idea too?" Havyn yanked his hand away from Ildar's and stood up to pace the clearing. His hands were fisted by his sides, and Severin could tell the young wizard was angry, but wasn't sure where he could find an outlet for it. As a slave, anger was an emotion he couldn't have afforded to show or he could well have ended up being beaten to within an inch of his life.

"No, the king had nothing to do with that. Aunt Xiana and the midwife feared for your safety after Eltan rejected your sister. My aunt bade my mother to take you somewhere safe. She intended to take you away from Oscia altogether, perhaps into Arcathia or Sadea and have you raised by a foster family. She didn't get that far because she was set upon by bandits on the road. They took you from her, leaving her for dead. The bandits had no idea they'd abducted a prince. My mother was disguised as a peasant so they thought they had a peasant baby. Slavers paid good money for boy slaves of any age."

"And my mother? What happened to my mother?" demanded Havyn.

"Eltan discovered the deception—that Xiana had borne him a son, but had sent him away that same evening. His mind broke and he strangled her."

Havyn paled again, but he didn't faint this time. Severin reckoned Havyn was too angry to faint. "How long have you known this? How long were you going to leave me to my fate as a slave?"

"I started dreaming of you a few months ago. That's why I went to the fortune-teller in the first place."

"And instead of finding me, you fell in love and ran away!" Havyn yelled, stalking off deeper into the trees. Severin made to go after him, but Ildar clutched at his hands.

"Leave him be, Severin. He needs to be alone right now."

"No, he doesn't," argued Severin, shaking off Ildar. He strode off into the woods in the same direction Havyn had taken. He found him quickly. Havyn was curled up at the base of a tree, his arms wrapped around his knees, sobbing into them.

Havyn looked up when Severin approached.

"I didn't want you to see me like this," said Havyn, hastily rubbing his eyes. "I don't want you to see me when I'm weak."

Severin gaped. Weak? "Havyn, you're the strongest person I've ever known." Severin knelt down beside him and tugged Havyn into his arms. Havyn's whole body shuddered with the effort of trying not to give into his tears. "You aren't weak, Havyn. Far from it. I can barely imagine having endured what you have. But you survived it, Havyn, and that makes you strong. My mother would say that emotions don't make you weak, but a lack of them does. Cry if you need to, I won't think any less of you."

Severin held Havyn tight while the apprentice wizard cried on his shoulder. Havyn sniffled and struggled to breathe at the same time, but he was glad that Havyn trusted him enough to weep in front of him. Nothing in the world existed except the two of them in each other's arms. Slowly, Havyn's weeping eased and he turned his head toward Severin.

"Do you think it's true? What Ythrin said?"

"It seems plausible enough," replied Severin. "I can see no reason why she would lie to you about it. What would she gain by telling you that you were the Oscian heir? She would lose her inheritance."

"I don't want it. I don't want to be a king!"

"Neither did I, but sometimes we don't always get what we want."

"No," said Havyn sadly.

"Do all Aldari have dark hair and violet eyes?" asked Severin.

"I don't know. Why do you ask?"

"I saw one in the woods at Aldford. She said she was a guardian of the pool but that they didn't normally walk in the world, just in certain places that they protect."

"Was she beautiful?"

"Very. At first I thought it was you."

"You think I'm beautiful?" Havyn asked, sounding surprised.

"I do."

"When...when I was a slave, I used to wish that I had a family who would come and rescue me. But now I've discovered who and what they are, and I want nothing to do with them. I don't want to be

Eltan's son, I don't. I can hardly bear it! I could sense how corrupted he was and it hurt every time I was in the same room with him. He's evil, Severin. His heart is dark." Havyn had worked himself up into such a state that he was soon weeping uncontrollably on Severin's shoulder. Severin did his best to comfort him.

"Ssh, Havyn. It's all right. No one has to know, we can keep it a secret if that's what you wish. It will be all right. You already have a family, Havyn. You'll always have a family in me."

Chapter Twenty One

Ythrin decided to go back and face her uncle so they travelled back to the port town of Beren, and the trip was without incident. Although she may have claimed to be his cousin, Havyn felt nothing in common with the princess. There was a coldness about her that seemed unnatural, as if she wasn't really living life, rather just watching other people, like she was observing performers in a play. Aviel was besotted with her, that much was obvious, but Havyn wasn't sure if the princess returned those feelings. He found it hard to read her at all and wondered if it was because she was part Aldari too.

Captain Kanmor and his ship, *Calira*, were still at the docks when they arrived, and as soon as he saw the party, he ran down to greet them, paying particular attention to Kelandra. Thankfully, Havyn was spared his attentions this time. Severin pressed his arms possessively around his waist when Kanmor passed them. The captain's men were busy packing and unpacking crates of stock they would be selling and putting on the supplies they'd need for their journey back home.

"Are you able to offer us passage back to Oscia, Captain Kanmor?" asked Kelandra, dismounting from her horse and accepting the kiss the captain gave her hand. Captain Kanmor seemed as enamoured of her as ever, and Havyn guessed that even if he didn't have room, the captain would have let them come aboard so that he could spend time with the pretty bodyguard.

Chayal looked most put out at all the attention Kanmor gave Kelandra. Havyn reached and tried to read Chayal, but couldn't and he knew it was because Chayal thought of Kelandra as a sister and wanted to look after her.

"Aye, we set sail on the evening tide. You almost missed us, but I'd be happy to take you back. This must be the princess?" Kanmor asked, raking his gaze over Ythrin, but he didn't linger. Soon, he turned back to Kelandra. Havyn was surprised, so, too, was Ythrin, if the glare she levelled at the captain's retreating back was anything to go by. Obviously, she wasn't used to being ignored.

"You were just about to offer my husband and I the use of your cabin, weren't you, Captain?" asked Ythrin haughtily, handing the reins of her horse to a passing sailor without even a thank you.

Kanmor turned and laughed. "Actually, I wasn't. The clue is in the name, see? *Captain's* cabin. I've ferried princes, kings, and queens before now, and none of them ousted me from my cabin. I'm not going to start now. You'll be fine in the guest quarters like everyone else."

"This is preposterous," she spluttered. If Havyn didn't know better, he was sure she was about to stamp her foot like a child throwing a tantrum

"Ythrin, the captain is Master of his own vessel," said Aviel, leading her away. They continued to argue while Havyn watched.

Chayal helped Ildar down from the horse, and when Havyn glanced back, he realised that the few days' ride back to port had made Ildar even more unwell than ever. His face was grey and haggard. It was the first time Havyn had thought of the man as old. He tottered on his legs when he reached the ground, but up until now, he had refused Havyn's offers to heal him. Ildar insisted he was fine. And even if wasn't, the man further claimed that he hadn't taught Havyn any healing spells, so he couldn't possibly help. Havyn didn't know how to tell his mentor that he didn't really need the spells. Now that he was attuned to magic, Havyn knew that his magic was within him. Magic wasn't some outside entity that relied on spells and ritual in order to be performed. If Ildar would only let him take a look, Havyn knew he could probably ease him, if not cure him outright.

"Are you all right, Havyn?" asked Severin from behind him.

"I'm just worried about Ildar. And the boat," Havyn replied, turning to face him. "I hate feeling sick."

"Perhaps the crossing won't be so bad this time," said Severin. "I don't want to get seasick again either. I don't think Ildar will be up to brewing ginger tea this time. He doesn't look good, does he?"

"No," said Havyn. "But he keeps insisting nothing is wrong."

"We'll get the palace healer to have a look at him once we get home."

"I wish we were there now," said Havyn.

"Me too, Havyn. Me too."

* * * *

Havyn bent over the ship's railing, the spray splashing against his face as he retched yet again. The sea was even rougher than last time, and he'd spent the past four days throwing up anything he tried to eat. Because he hadn't eaten much, nothing but bile and sour spittle made an appearance. He felt awful and just wished they were off the ship already. This time, Severin hadn't gotten sick at all, but spent his days shadowing Havyn and rubbing his back, mumbling soothing nonsense while Havyn was sick yet again. Ildar was bedridden in his cabin, and Captain Kanmor had finally worn the wizard down and got the ship's cook to look at him. They didn't have a proper healer, but the cook was well versed in herb lore. Like Havyn had suspected, it was Ildar's heart. Due to his advanced age, it wasn't working properly any more, and he needed to take it much easier than he had been.

At least they didn't have the worry about Ildar catching them together because Ildar was too unwell to leave their shared cabin. The bowels of the boat made him even sicker, so Havyn spent most of his time on deck. If he hadn't been so cold, if he'd had Severin to cuddle up to, he'd have probably slept out there. Even with Ildar indisposed, he knew neither of them could risk anything so blatant.

He saw little of his cousin and her husband, much to his relief. Havyn found her rather odd, and wondered if everyone else thought him odd because of his Aldari heritage.

"Some wine, Havyn?" Severin asked him, handing him a linen handkerchief so he could wipe his mouth.

"I'd like some water," Havyn croaked. Scraped so raw it seemed his insides had been torn through his throat.

"I'll see if there's any to spare, if not, will you take the wine?"

Havyn nodded, anything to take the horrible taste away, but he knew wine on an empty stomach was not the best thing for him when he was so ill. He leaned over the rail and stared at the waves as the boat sailed through them. Was it his imagination or was the sea getting even choppier? Large waves rose up, slapping against the hull, the momentum made the boat sway even more. Havyn groaned and gripped the rail with white knuckled hands.

The sky darkened, black clouds obscuring the sun. From the feel of the air, he knew a storm wasn't far off. That was all they needed. Lightning forked across the sky in the distance followed by rumbles of thunder. The waves were getting wilder, some even rising as high as the deck, soaking all those who were there, including Havyn. Severin wobbled from side to side as he tried to make his way back to Havyn, a wooden beaker gripped tightly in his hand, the other hand covering the top so as not to allow the contents to spill.

"I managed to get you some water," said Severin, offering him the beaker. Havyn took it and sipped. The water was warm, but at that moment, he didn't care. It was the sweetest water he'd ever tasted and he downed it all in a matter of moments. "Thanks," Havyn replied, handing him back the beaker.

"Would you like something to eat? There's some bread and jam."

Havyn shook his head. "No thanks. Just the thought of food makes me want to be sick again."

"I don't like the look of that storm," said Severin. "It's coming closer."

"Ildar! You should be resting," scolded Kelandra and they both turned to see the bodyguard try and get Ildar back to the steps that led to the guest quarters.

"I'm needed here," protested Ildar, making his way over to them in a zigzag pattern as he tried to keep his feet with the rocking and rolling of the boat. "Havyn, I need you, too. Come with me. I need to show you how to calm the storm. This way, quickly now," said Ildar, holding onto his staff with one hand and grabbing hold of Havyn with the other. If he noticed that Severin and Havyn were standing closer to each other than was considered polite, he never mentioned it.

Havyn followed the wizard up to the prow of the ship where they stood in the 'v' of the railings. The boat rose high up in the air, and then back down, making Havyn's stomach roil once more. The sails flapped loudly in the wind. It was difficult to hear anything over the roar of the wind and the turmoil of the water.

"You must imagine yourself as the sea," said Ildar. "Imagine yourself calm and serene like a sheet of glass. There isn't a ripple. Your surface is as smooth as that same glass. There are no waves, no wind. Close your eyes and concentrate."

Havyn did as he was bid, but when he closed his eyes, he couldn't get a fixed position on the horizon and it made his nausea worse. He sank to his knees, unable to make it to the side of the boat. Clutching his abdomen, he vomited once more onto the wooden deck. It was watery and sour, and the smell wasn't helping him feel better.

"I want off. I want off!" Havyn sobbed to the wind. He couldn't endure this much longer. Panic rose at the idea of three more weeks of this. He didn't know how he was going to be able to bear it. Ildar looked beyond him and beckoned someone forward.

"Severin, hold Havyn up, he needs to be standing for the spell to work," said Ildar.

Severin's arms came around his waist, tugging him up and holding Havyn securely against his chest.

"I can't do it if I close my eyes," said Havyn. "It makes me sick."

"Very well, lad. Try it with your eyes open, it was just a way to help you concentrate and clear your mind. I don't think your eyes need to be closed, but that's the way I've always done it. Remember now, think of something calm."

Havyn nodded, but then regretted even that small movement when it made him light headed. Tears dripped down his cheeks, but the wind dried them before they fell far. Severin's arms were strong around him, keeping him safe. Havyn kept that knowledge close to his heart. The storm couldn't harm them when Severin was here, and he did as Ildar had suggested, imagining the sea as calm as glass. No waves, no wind. But they needed the wind for the sails. He'd seen the oars, but knew they would get to their destination that much quicker if the wind caught the sails. So some wind then, but not a storm. No rough water. Smooth. Smooth. Smooth.

At first, Havyn thought it would never happen, that the storm would never calm. He shivered in his wet clothes, his teeth chattering as the wind buffeted against them. He could tell Severin was struggling to keep him upright, but not once did Havyn doubt him. Severin would hold onto him no matter what.

"It's easing," said Ildar, staring back at Havyn and smiling. "Well done, Havyn. Well done!"

The world around Havyn continued to spin; Ildar's voice seemed to be coming from a long way off. Spots danced in front of his eyes as he sagged against Severin and let the darkness claim him.

Chapter Twenty Two

Despite never having allowed it before, and much to Ythrin's chagrin, once Captain Kanmor discovered how ill Havyn was, and how instrumental he'd been in arranging the weather to get them back home, the captain allowed Havyn to rest in his cabin rather than in the guest quarters. At least it was above deck and had some windows so Havyn could get some fresh air. Severin spent nearly every moment with Havyn. He found that he wished he'd paid more attention to Ildar when the wizard had been trying to teach him the more common treatments for minor ailments. It was his mother who had the skills with healing, not him.

"There isn't a lot more I can do, Lord Severin," said the cook on the fifth day of Havyn's illness. Severin wished they were back at the palace and Havyn in the hands of a proper healer. Havyn was having hallucinations, shouting and screaming at people who weren't there. Havyn didn't seem to know that Severin was even in the room with him.

At turns, Havyn both shivered and felt as if he were close to a burning fire. The sheets had to be freshened three times a day because the cook insisted that damp sheets would have made his condition worse. They had no luck getting much food into him, but sometimes he was lucid enough to drink some water. Severin knew the water wasn't going to last much longer. Already, Havyn had been drinking more than his ration, but no one begrudged him, considering how ill he was. Severin was sure it must have been something other than simple seasickness, but he had no idea what, nor how to help him.

Severin never left Havyn's side except to relieve himself, he was too worried. Sometimes the cook came by with some bread soaked in milk, which they tried to get Havyn to eat. As soon as the food hit his throat, he retched and it was brought straight back up again.

"How is he today?" asked the cook, peeking his head in the door.

Severin rinsed out the cloth he'd been mopping Havyn's brow with and shook his head. "Still the same, he's burning up. We need to get his temperature down somehow."

"A cold bath?" the cook suggested, eyeing the captain's wooden bathtub, which sat by the window. "We could haul up some seawater. There's not enough fresh left."

"It's worth a try," said Severin, sinking down on the stool next to the bed. The embroidered quilt was tucked up at the foot of the bed, but Havyn was too warm for anything other than a sheet on top of him.

"I'll get some of the men on it right away," said the cook, leaving Severin and Havyn alone once more. Havyn had received quite a few visitors while he lay so ill. Chayal and Kelandra, the sailors and the captain, and even Ildar, who had been feeling much better now, but not recovered enough to do any healing spells for Havyn. Aviel sometimes visited, too, but there was no sign of Havyn's royal cousin.

On the bed, Havyn groaned, flinging his arms about, like he was fighting off some invisible attacker. His shirt was drenched in sweat, and his hair stuck to his face in sweaty clumps. Severin lifted the cloth and smoothed it across his forehead, Havyn whimpered when he did so.

"Ssh, Havyn. It's going to be all right. We'll be home soon."

If only they could have gotten a hold of one of those ancient portal stones, they could get back to Arcathia instantly without having to worry about facing Eltan at all. Severin hoped Ythrin didn't mention to her uncle that she'd found his son after all these years. And Eltan! Killing his wife! The man must have some strange madness. Severin didn't want to remain in his company for longer than necessary. As soon as they saw Ythrin back to the castle, they'd head straight back to Arcathia and then home.

Severin stared at the young wizard so ill on the bed and sighed. Even though Ythrin had now married Aviel, nothing had really changed for him, Arcathia still needed an heir, and he still needed to get married in order to gain a legitimate one. It was even worse now, knowing how deeply he felt for Havyn. To give that up and marry someone else? Severin didn't want to do it. He wondered if Ildar was right and that the Aldari could change their shape or their sex? If that was the case, he could marry Havyn, couldn't he? The fact still remained; Severin didn't desire women and never had. All that softness and flowery scent did nothing for him. It was hard chests he dreamed of, muscles firm beneath the skin, not velvet folds.

The cook returning with lots of other sailors behind him brought him out of his ruminations. The sailors hefted buckets of water, which they tipped into the bath, one after the other. It seemed to be a never-ending stream of people, when one man had finished, another took his place and poured his own bucket in.

Once the bath was over halfway full, the cook waved them all out and came over to help Severin lift Havyn to the bathtub.

"Shirt on or off?" asked the cook, taking hold of Havyn's legs.

"On," said Severin, wanting to preserve Havyn's dignity as much as possible, although he didn't think the cook was interested in Havyn as anything other than his patient. Severin lifted Havyn, and between the two of them, they managed to get Havyn into the tub where he promptly shrieked with the shock of such cold water. Havyn struggled to get out of their grasp. But they held firm and kept him in the water until he started shivering uncontrollably and his teeth chattered.

Once out, Severin wrapped him in a towel and removed the shirt from underneath him so the cook saw nothing. He knew how modest the apprentice was. Severin himself had never seen Havyn completely naked and he didn't want the first time to be when he was so sick. The cook got another towel, wrapped it around Havyn's shoulders, and dabbed his hair dry.

Severin led the still shivering Havyn back over to the bed and pushed him to sit down on it. The young wizard was so thin, his skin stretched taut over his frame, and his eyes were hollowed with purple shadows under them. The bruise-like colouring reminded Severin of the day he'd hit Havyn in his grief and confusion over his father's death. How could he have done such a thing to him? Severin knew the guilt about that would never leave him. He vowed then and there that he would never allow anything to hurt Havyn ever again.

"S-s-Severin?" Havyn stammered, glancing around the captain's cabin as though he'd never seen it before.

"Thank the Raven!" said Severin, caressing his cheek. "You're fine, Havyn. You're going to be fine."

* * * *

When the ship docked at Fair Haven, Ildar and Havyn remained weak, so Kanmor sent one of his men off to find them a cart so that they wouldn't need to walk or ride to the castle. Severin didn't want to go anywhere near it, and he certainly didn't want Eltan anywhere near Havyn. What if he discovered Havyn was his son and he demanded Havyn stay in Oscia?

Once they and their supplies were unloaded, the sailor returned with a wooden cart attached to two sturdy looking horses. Ythrin glanced disdainfully at it, wrinkling her nose at the smell that lingered, probably from the animals that it had once transported.

"We should send to the castle for a proper carriage," she insisted. "It should only take a few hours."

"We want to be on our way home in a few hours," said Severin. "We are escorting you both back to the castle and then we are leaving. We've done what King Eltan asked of us. We found you, our duty is done."

"Very well," said Ythrin. She sighed. "But I'm sure my uncle will want to reward you somehow. Aren't you even going to stay for a feast?"

Remembering the food only too well from the last Oscian feast, Severin shook his head.

"Let's go," said Severin, leading Havyn by the elbow, and then boosting him up into the cart, while Chayal helped Ildar over the other side of it.

Kelandra said goodbye to the captain. She tried to get him to accept a bag of gold coins for all of his help.

He wouldn't take them, but thrust them back into her hand. "I've already been paid a fair price. You owe me nothing," insisted the captain. "Except perhaps a goodbye kiss?" He winked at her and Kelandra laughed.

"You are a rogue, but I think I can manage that."

Severin looked away as they kissed, feeling a little embarrassed at seeing them like that. He'd never really thought of Kelandra as a woman until this trip. She'd just been his friend and his bodyguard. It was good to see her so happy though.

Kelandra was almost skipping when she returned to them. Every so often she'd break into a broad grin. Severin stayed with Ildar and Havyn in the cart, leaving the others to ride, leading the way back to the castle.

When they approached, they saw the black flags flying from the battlements as well as black banners hanging over all the walls they could see. The chancellor awaited their arrival when they entered the courtyard flanked by two men-at-arms, all of them wearing black armbands.

"Princess Ythrin," said the chancellor, bowing low and helping her down from her horse. "I am sorry to be the bearer of bad tidings.

Your uncle passed away three weeks ago. He has been interred in the castle crypt."

"He's dead?" Ythrin asked, with as much curiosity as if she was enquiring about the weather. Beside Severin, Havyn stiffened. If Ildar hadn't been there, Severin would have squeezed his hand or offered some other form of comfort. Havyn may not have wanted Eltan to be his father or even liked the man, but the fact remained, Eltan had been his father. Perhaps Havyn was feeling some sort of grief.

"And his heir? Did he leave word?" she asked.

"He did. Your husband is to be the next King of Oscia." The chancellor turned to Severin and bowed to the cart. "Welcome, King Severin of Oscia."

Severin tried not to laugh, but Ythrin beat him to it. "Severin will not be my husband," she said. "That is what his word says? That my husband is to be the next king? Was a name mentioned?"

"No, your highness. Just that your husband is to be named king."

Ythrin turned to Aviel, sitting astride the horse beside her own. "Well then, Lord Joran, I give you my husband. King Aviel of Oscia."

Chapter Twenty Three

Havyn awoke to gentle but firm hands caressing his forehead. Eyes still closed, he arched toward the touch and breathed out a name. "Severin." Havyn's mind was filled with fragments of half-remembered thoughts and dreams. He still wasn't sure if any of it had been real. Sea monsters, princesses, storms, death, and illness. Throughout it all, there had been one constant, one thing that kept him going. One person who had never wavered. Severin had always been there for him. Eltan, his father, was dead now. For so many years he'd thought of himself as an orphan, now he was one.

"Severin?" he queried again, trying to open his eyes. His eyelids were so heavy, like they had been weighted down with lead. Once he did manage to get them open, he had to blink rapidly at the brightness filling the room. This wasn't their chamber at Fair Haven castle. The sunlight had barely penetrated the window holes there.

"Severin, close the shutters," said a female voice close to his ear, as she caressed his brow once more. It hadn't been Severin who was touching him, but his mother. No wonder the touch had seemed so familiar.

"What happened?" The last thing Havyn remembered was being cajoled into attending King Aviel's coronation feast before they were allowed to take their leave of Oscia. He didn't remember much after that.

"You've been very ill, Havyn," said Yinare. "We feared we might lose you. Severin and the others brought you home, but you've been unwell for weeks now. They thought at first you were getting better, but you took ill again in Oscia. You've had such a high fever that you have been delirious. You probably don't remember a lot yet."

"Ildar. Is Master Ildar all right?" Havyn distinctly remembered the wizard hadn't been at all well on that journey either.

"Ildar is fine, Havyn. He has had plenty of rest and the healers have made him up some medicine, he'll need to take it every day, but he is as good as new."

Severin returned to the bed once he'd closed the shutters, sealing the room in semi-darkness. "Now, how about you?" asked Yinare. "Are you hungry?"

"Not really," Havyn admitted. "I feel strange."

"Strange? In what way? Sick?"

Havyn thought for a moment. "No. More light headed, I think."

"Well, that's to be expected. You've been lying in bed for quite some time and you've only had nutrition potions. We'll get you sitting up and some food into you. That should make you feel better soon. Severin, give me a hand," ordered Yinare as she stood up and began pulling at Havyn's pillows. Severin took hold of Havyn underneath his shoulders, hoisting him upright. The room spun wildly, and nausea threatened to overwhelm him, but Havyn managed to damp it down by swallowing rapidly. His throat felt raw, as if he'd been swallowing sand or gravel for days.

"The sickness should pass in a moment, Havyn," Yinare assured him. "I think we'll try you with some soup to start with. Severin, can you keep him company while I inform the kitchens?"

"Of course, Mother," said Severin, kissing her cheek.

"Havyn, there is some water here for you. I'll let Severin pour it."

"Thank you," Havyn croaked. His limbs felt like water rather than flesh and bone.

"You're very welcome. I'll be back soon."

Yinare closed the bedroom door with a soft click behind her. When Havyn's eyes got used to the gloom, he realised he was in his bedroom at the palace of Ravensfell. Part of the apartments he shared with Ildar. It seemed like Severin had been with him for quite some time. Severin poured him a cup of water which Havyn sipped gradually. His hand shook so much he was surprised most of it didn't end up over the bed or the floor.

"What if Ildar finds you here?" asked Havyn. Not that he wanted Severin to go, far from it, but he didn't want to suffer the wizard's wrath either.

"He already knows," said Severin.

"Knows?"

"About us," explained Severin. "About how I feel about you. I thought I was going to lose you, Havyn and I couldn't bear it. I can't imagine my life without you in it. I want you to be my bond-mate, Havyn."

"Your what?"

"It's like a marriage, but a bonding can be between two men or two women. You would be treated as my spouse and I yours. It's one way we can be together."

"But I can't give you an heir," said Havyn.

"You won't need to. My heir is already conceived," said Severin, smiling. Havyn felt as if he'd just been doused in a bucket of ice-cold water.

"You've lain with a woman?" Havyn's mind tormented him with the image of Lady Kessarie finally getting her clutches on Severin, the two of them entwined on a large bed. Laughing at him, at how foolish he'd been to fall in love.

Severin laughed. "By the Raven, no! I don't desire women, I never have. Do you remember Captain Kanmor?"

Havyn nodded.

"Kelandra has been my best friend for years, Havyn and she knows that I am not at all interested in women as bed partners. Kelandra's pregnant, the baby is the captain's, but he is not interested in raising a child. They have agreed that we can adopt the child."

"But why would they to agree to such a thing? To letting someone else raise their child? Wouldn't Kelandra want to raise her own baby?"

"Kelandra is pleased that she is having a baby, but she also wants to remain with the Daughters as my bodyguard. She would have to give one of them up. The baby will be ours, Havyn, but Kelandra will get to see her son or daughter grow up. She can be a favourite aunt instead of a full time mother."

"And the captain? He hardly knows us, why would he agree to such a thing?" Havyn couldn't imagine that if he had his own child he want to give it up to someone else, but then he hadn't been brought up as royalty with all of the attendant worries about heirs.

"Captain Kanmor is dying, Havyn. He's been ill for a long time. He had never intended to have any children because he knew he wouldn't be around to look after them. It was a bit of a surprise when he discovered Kelandra was pregnant. Knowing that we can adopt the child and that Kelandra will still be part of the child's life will give him more peace of mind. He has no objections to the adoption and has already signed the papers to that effect. So has Kelandra. All that remains is for us to agree and sign too."

"I see," said Havyn. That made a bit more sense. "What if it's a girl? Will everyone still want you to have a son too?" Havyn imagined lots of women trying to bed Severin in order to conceive his next heir and his heart hurt at the thought. "I'm the king, I've changed the law so that the heir can be a boy or a girl, and to make it legal for an adopted child to become Arcathia's heir."

"And you want me to be with you?" Havyn could hardly believe it. Sometimes he had allowed himself to dream of such a moment, but that's all that it had felt like. A dream. Not something that would ever happen to him.

"You're of royal blood too, Havyn. It would be unusual, since I don't ever intend to take a wife, but there is no law that prohibits me having a male consort. I love you, Havyn. I've never felt about anyone else the way I do about you. I'm yours, if you'll have me."

"Severin! Oh, Severin," sobbed Havyn, reaching his arms around Severin's neck and holding him close. "Do you mean it?"

"I do, Havyn, I do." Severin pressed a kiss against his hair, wrapping his arms around Havyn's waist and holding him tight.

"The queen sent a tray," said Lady Kessarie by the doorway. Havyn hadn't even heard her knock and wondered if she had just barged in without knocking.

"I'll take that," said Severin, taking the tray from her and settling it on Havyn's lap. Severin stirred the soup, a thick vegetable broth, and lifted it to his mouth to blow on it to cool it.

"*No!*" She slapped the spoon from his hand, hot droplets landing on Havyn's sheets.

Severin gripped her wrist, glowering down at her "What did you do? What did you put in it? Poison? Did you intend to poison him? Answer me, or by all the gods I'll have the flesh flayed from your back before I hang you as a traitor!"

"Not poison, no," she whimpered.

"Havyn, is she telling the truth?"

"It's not poison," said Havyn, trying to sense the answer from her. "It's a love philtre."

"A love philtre? You attempted to give Havyn a love philtre? By all that's holy, why?"

"I knew you wouldn't want to be with him if he was already soiled," she said simply.

"And you were going to be the one who plucked him, were you? What? You hoped I would catch you together and blame it all on Havyn for betraying me?"

Her silence was answer enough. "Chayal!" Severin roared, still holding onto Kessarie. The tall bodyguard entered the bedroom, glancing at Havyn, then to Severin and Kessarie.

"Take her to the garrison cells," said Severin. "Let the judge decide her fate, but for me, I advocate banishment."

"No. Please, Severin. I did it for you! You're the king because of me. I should be your queen!"

"How dare you address me so informally, madam. Take her away." Severin let go of her wrists as though her touch burned him.

Chayal produced a length of rope from one of the many pockets lining his breeches and bound her hands. Havyn couldn't help but remember all the times his hands had been bound as he'd been brought out onto the auction blocks, and although he did feel some sympathy for her, he would be glad to see her go.

"I killed your father for you!" she shrieked. "I paid them to kill him. I knew how much you hated him!"

Severin stared hard at her. "I never hated my father," he said quietly. "You are doubly condemned out of your own mouth. To murder the king is treason. You are dead to me."

Kessarie was still shrieking and sobbing when Chayal led her away.

"Is it true?" asked Havyn softly.

"What?"

"That you wouldn't want me if I wasn't a virgin? What if I'd been a body slave? Would you still have wanted me?"

"Of course I would!" Severin said. Havyn could sense the truth from him. He didn't know why it had worried him so much when he knew how much Severin cared for him.

"Ah, how's the patient?" came Ildar's voice from the door. He looked a lot better than the last time Havyn had seen him, with a rosy flush to his cheeks and a spring in his step that Havyn had seldom seen.

Havyn's heart faltered a little as he looked at the wizard and lowered his head, shame almost choked him.

"I'm sorry, Ildar. I know I must have disappointed you."

Ildar strode over to the bed and patted his hand. "Hush now, lad. There's no shame in love, I'm just an old man who let it pass me by when I had the chance. You and Severin belong together. Any blind man can see that. I'll just be sorry to lose my apprentice."

"You're not going to teach me anymore?" asked Havyn. "I still have a lot to learn."

"You would still like to learn from me? Even though you are far more powerful?"

"There's not much point in having power if you don't know how to use it," explained Havyn. He enjoyed their lessons and didn't want to give them up.

"Well, then, I'd better arrange some classes for you when you're well again, hadn't I?"

"Thank you, Ildar."

"My pleasure, lad. My pleasure," Ildar grinned at him before taking his leave.

Once he was gone, Severin removed the food from Havyn's lap, set it down on the floor and climbed onto the bed. He wrapped Havyn up in his arms and kissed his hair.

"How does an autumn ceremony sound?" asked Severin.

"When's autumn?"

"About two weeks away."

"It sounds wonderful."

"That it does, Havyn. That it does."

Chapter Twenty Four

Standing in a platform in the middle of his bedroom two weeks later, Havyn was reminded of the day Severin had decided he needed lots of new clothes. There were new clothes today, too, but this time it was different. These were the clothes he would be wearing to his bonding ceremony at the temple. Bonded to Severin as equals, not as a slave. Havyn worried that he didn't quite know how to act as an equal. First he'd been a slave, then an apprentice. There was always someone else who had power over him, he'd never been his own person and he wasn't quite sure how to be.

"Havyn? Are you all right?" asked Yinare as she smoothed down his ceremonial robe. It was silver, threaded through with gold designs of flowers and animals. Havyn couldn't quite believe it was himself staring back when he caught sight of his reflection in the looking glass.

He was still a little on the thin side, his appetite hadn't quite recovered to what it was before his illness, and in the past few days, Iri, the royal tailor had adjusted his robe so that it would fit better. His hair had grown a bit, now it hung loose past his shoulders, the dark curls becoming more like waves the longer it grew.

"Just a bit nervous," said Havyn.

"That's to be expected, dear."

Kelandra returned from the bathroom, still looking pale. Havyn remembered his own days of throwing up only too well, and he couldn't help but feel sympathetic toward her. When he thought about how she was going through this to give him and Severin a child, it made Havyn admire her even more.

"Ildar has left you some more ginger tea, Kelandra," said Yinare, pointing to the bedside table.

"Oh, thank you," said Kelandra, sitting down on the bed and taking a sip. "I feel much better already. It's better out than in, I suppose."

"There," said Yinare, standing back and admiring Havyn as if he'd been a doll. Truth to tell, he felt a bit like one this morning because according to Arcathian custom, neither he nor Severin were to do anything for themselves this morning. Much to his mortification, Havyn had been bathed by some of the palace servants, who had bathed him with brisk efficiency and didn't pay attention to his indignant protests that he was quite capable of bathing himself. After that, Yinare and Kelandra had dressed his hair, placing white and blue flowers all through his locks before Iri had placed his wedding finery on him.

Also, according to custom, the ceremonial robes were worn with nothing underneath, not even stockings or underlinens. He and Severin would make their way to the temple in bare feet. That part hadn't worried Havyn, but it did feel strange to have nothing between his skin and the material of his robe. The robe had laces at the front, from the neck to the waist, but once tightened properly, no flesh was visible.

"You look gorgeous, Havyn," said Kelandra, standing up and perusing Havyn as much as the queen and the tailor were doing. "Severin is a very lucky man."

"I'm the lucky one," said Havyn.

* * * *

Severin stood by the North altar in the temple, Chayal and Ildar by his side. The priestess stood in front of them, her masked face visible by the flickering fires from the other altars. His hair was loose today, as was the custom for getting married and it was annoying him. He kept reaching back to tie it up, but Ildar and Chayal kept staying his hands. He hopped from foot to foot while they waited for Havyn and the others to arrive. What if Havyn had changed his mind? What if this wasn't what he wanted after all?

Cheers went up from outside. Severin turned toward the colonnade to see the citizens throwing flowers in front of the procession, Havyn at its head, the queen and Kelandra flanking him. Havyn looked like he couldn't quite believe this was happening, but when he caught sight of Severin waiting for him, his smile lit up his whole face. It was as if he'd swallowed the sun and it blazed from his skin.

Severin returned the smile, feeling his own heart thud against his chest as he anticipated tonight and the consummation of their marriage. Havyn hadn't been well enough yet for anything more than kisses, but Severin knew that they were both ready for more now. It was just a pity that they were both quite as innocent as the other. They'd have to muddle their way through somehow. Severin guessed it would be fun finding out.

Once Havyn reached him, the priestess took his left hand and placed it in Severin's.

"We are gathered here today to witness the bonding of King Severin of Arcathia and Prince Havyn of Oscia. If there is anyone present who believes there is any lawful impediment to this joining, let them speak now or be forever silent."

There was a pause. Severin and Havyn both held their breath, but no arguments were forthcoming from any of the assembled guests.

"Severin, you may speak your vows," said the priestess.

"I, Severin, do take you Havyn to be my bond-mate. In good times and in bad, in sickness and in health, for all the days of our lives. I promise to protect you, to hear no word spoken against you, and I promise to be faithful to your forever. All that I am, I give to you. All that I have, I share with you. You are my world, and your happiness means more to me than my own."

"Now you, Havyn."

"I, Havyn, do take you Severin to be my bond-mate. In good times and in bad, in sickness and in health, for all the days of our lives. I promise to protect you, to hear no work spoken against you, and I promise to be faithful to you forever. All that I am, I give to you. All that I have, I share with you. You are my world and your happiness means more to me than my own."

The priestess lifted up a silver goblet of water from the altar and held it to Severin's lips. "Drink both of you from the one cup to show that you are now one rather than two."

Severin drank the water before the priestess pressed the goblet to Havyn's lips.

"Who blesses this union?" asked the priestess once she'd set the goblet down again.

Yinare stepped forward and wrapped white ribbon around their wrists, binding them together. "I do. I bless you both with long life and happiness."

Chayal went next, adding a blue ribbon. "I bless this union with wealth and fortune."

Kelandra added her red ribbon. "I bless this union with children." There were a few murmurs of surprise at that, but nothing overly vociferous.

Ildar took his place after Kelandra, placing a dove grey ribbon around their hands. "I bless this union with wisdom and serenity."

The priestess took hold of the ends of the ribbons and unravelled them slightly so that she could ease their palms apart. Another priestess stepped forward, knelt down before her and held a dagger across her palms. The priestess took the dagger and scored a line through Severin's palm and then Havyn's. With their palms still bleeding, the priestess pressed both of their hands together so that their blood mingled.

"By blood you are both bound, only by blood can you be unbound. May the Raven Mother bless this union and give you long life and happiness. You have been bound according to our laws and customs. From this day henceforth, you are not two, but one. You may kiss each other."

Havyn's tongue peeked out from between lips the colour of ripe strawberries, glistening as he licked them. Severin closed his eyes and leaned down, pressing his lips softly against Havyn's. The kiss went on for quite some time, and when Severin pulled away, Havyn looked as dazed as Severin felt.

Cheers erupted from the assembled guests and as the priestess untied their ribbons, he and Havyn were almost crushed under the onslaught of well-wishers.

Ythrin was there along with Aviel and she hugged both of them, surprising Havyn if the shocked look on his face was anything to go by.

"Congratulations, cousin. And to you, Severin. Our kingdoms have been joined after all, no?" she smiled and shook his hand.

"Indeed. Thank you for accepting our invitation."

"It was the least we could do," said Aviel. "My mother has offered you both a reading as a wedding gift."

Severin glanced at his new bond-mate and they both shook their heads. "No, I think we've heard enough of the future."

The guests suddenly parted and Severin saw the Oracle walking toward them with a wrapped bundle in her arms. She stopped by him, as if she knew exactly where he was, despite being blind. "King Severin, may I ask your blessing on my daughter?" she asked, offering him the wrapped bundle. Severin took the baby from her, seeing a thatch of dark hair beneath the blankets and smiled, remembering holding a dark-haired infant in one of his visions. It hadn't been his own child at all.

"I would be honoured, Gracious One," said Severin. "May she live a long life filled with love and joy."

"Thank you," said the Oracle, taking the newborn back to her arms and returning to an unknown part of the temple.

Kanmor gave Havyn and Severin hearty hugs, the big man seemed out of his depth on dry land. Severin guessed he would soon be returning to his real home, the sea. It was hard to believe that such a strong man was dying, but Severin knew that not every illness left visible traces. Since so many people had wanted to see them bonded, instead of the wedding feast taking place in the dining halls of the castle, Yinare had decided it should take place in the market square so that all the inhabitants of Ravensfell could attend and get a free meal into the bargain.

When the others were heading out toward the market square, Severin held onto Havyn's arm and looked back at the temple, where he saw one of the priestesses removing her mask. Severin had never seen any priestess without her mask before, and he watched in awe as her face was revealed. His heart thudded wildly against his chest because it was a face he had seen before. The violet eyes were unmistakable.

The woman held her fingers to her lips and Severin nodded. He would keep their secret, as he suspected his father had kept the secret before him. It was no wonder they wore masks, their true identity cloaked. The Aldari had never left them. Rather they were hiding in plain sight, still protecting them after all this time. Severin smiled, bowing to her before tugging Havyn outside.

All the market stalls had been removed to make way for tables dressed with white linen. Those very tables groaned with the weight of the food placed upon them. Other surfaces held plates, goblets, and cutlery, enabling the guests to choose their food and mill about as much as they wanted. There were tureens of different soups, platters of carved meats, bowls of steaming vegetables, and salads, cakes, and desserts by the thousands.

Seeing all the crowds, Severin knew he didn't want to spend the next few hours trying to make small talk with thousands of people he didn't know. He certainly didn't want to make any speeches.

"Chayal, can you get us back to the palace?" asked Severin. All the main roads were blocked with people.

"Severin, you have to be at the feast," protested Kelandra.

"No, I don't. I'm the king. I can miss the feast if I want."

Chayal guffawed loudly. "Aye, I can get you back. Deciding to get a head start on the bedding ceremony?"

"Something like that," Severin grinned, taking hold of Havyn's hand and following Chayal down a myriad of lots and side alleyways that took them to the back door of the palace kitchens.

* * * *

Once in Severin's bedchamber, the nervousness that Havyn had been feeling all day increased tenfold. The large bed had been draped with garlands of wild flowers all along the posts and headboard, making the room smell more like a meadow than a bedroom.

The shutters were already closed. Candles and lamps had been lit, giving everything a soft glow. There was a table and two chairs by the closed window with a bowl of fruit, two crystal goblets, and a decanter of wine in the middle of it.

"Ah, excellent!" said Severin, bounding over and pouring them out a measure of red wine. "To us." He touched his glass to Havyn's.

"To us," echoed Havyn, taking a drink of the fruity flavoured wine.

Once Severin had drunk his fill of the wine, he plucked the goblet from Havyn's hand and pulled Havyn tight against him.

"I've missed you," Severin sighed against his hair before leaning to kiss him once more. This was no soft press of lips like back at the temple. This was a devouring, a claiming as they crushed the breath from each other.

Havyn could taste the wine on Severin's lips and tried to relax into it, after all they had kissed before and it was nothing to be scared of. He didn't know how long they stood there in the middle of the room, both seeming as reticent as the other to get to the next stage despite their staffs rising with passion. Severin pulled away first, gasping for breath.

"Are you as nervous as I am?"

"Probably more," admitted Havyn, glancing at the vial of oil on the bedside table.

"Well, we'll just have to get you more relaxed, won't we?" asked Severin, grinning. "I think we're both a bit overdressed, aren't we?" Severin began to untie the laces holding his robe closed. Havyn found his gaze drawn to those hands as they undid the laces as deftly as any of the palace maids. He shuddered with desire when he remembered those hands on his bare skin.

"You too," said Severin. "I want to see you."

Havyn's hands trembled while he undid his own laces. They held their robes closed with their hands once the laces had been undone, unwilling to be the first to get naked. "Together," suggested Severin and they both let go of their robes at the same time.

As soon as Severin's robes dropped, Havyn stared at the sparse, fair hair at Severin's groin, so different to his own smoothness. Almost without conscious thought, Havyn reached out and trailed his hand through the nest of curls. Severin moaned and clung to his arm, as if his legs could no longer hold him up.

Once he had recovered himself, Severin stood and before Havyn could even voice a protest, Severin had scooped him up in his arms and carried him over to the bed. When the king placed him upon it, Severin lay down the full of length of him and kissed him passionately, desperately. There were wild kisses, both of them biting, teeth clacking together, tongues tangling as they tried to suck each other's souls out through their mouths.

Havyn stopped kissing Severin, turning his body so that he could reach the vial of oil. He handed it to Severin, pleased to note that although his hands were still shaking, it was from desire and not nervousness this time.

"Are you sure, Havyn?" Severin asked, kissing his neck. "I've heard it can hurt a bit."

"I know you wouldn't mean it," said Havyn. "I want this. I want you, Severin. Take me, I'm yours."

Severin removed the lid from the vial of oil before dipping his fingers in and coating them liberally. "Lift your legs," he suggested and once Havyn had done so, he proceeded to prepare him with slick fingers. They slid in so easily that Havyn never had time to panic that they might not fit, and although he was a bit nervous, he wasn't scared at all. "You need to relax around them."

It was only when the third finger breached him that Havyn had any twinges of pain. He remembered what Severin said about relaxing and took a few deep breaths as Severin eased his fingers in. Severin pushed his fingers in and out of Havyn and then as he pushed in again, he hit something inside Havyn that had him almost arching off the bed in ecstasy. "What was that? There's something inside. Oh, please, do that again!" begged Havyn, arching his head up and glancing at Severin.

The desire Havyn saw on Severin' face was nothing short of electrifying. Havyn's heart raced and his hips began to meet Severin' thrust for thrust, impaling himself on those fingers.

"Does it feel good?" asked Severin

Good didn't even begin to describe it. Havyn had no words for the pleasure coursing through his veins in waves. His staff was hard and aching, and Havyn wanted to feel Severin's staff pressing inside him, splitting him open. Claiming Havyn as his own. He was aching with want. "Now! Oh please, gods now!" gabbled Havyn. "In me, I want you in me!"

Severin leaned up and kissed Havyn's neck while he removed his fingers. Havyn turned his head so that Severin' kisses fell on his mouth instead. Neither of them mentioned any other position, Havyn knew he needed to do this face to face and Severin just nodded.

Havyn watched with hungry eyes as Severin stroked oil over his shaft. Soon that staff was going to be inside him. Severin was going to be inside him and Havyn could hardly wait. His hips shifted restlessly on the bed while he waited for Severin to finish rubbing the lubricant over himself. Severin pulled Havyn's legs apart. Havyn had been used to pleasuring himself for quite some time now, but being with someone else made the sensations seem so much more. Severin's caresses were different to his own touches and kindled desire deep within him.

"Ready?" asked Severin as he knelt underneath Havyn and tugged his legs toward him.

"Yes," gasped Havyn. He thought he might die if Severin didn't do something soon.

Severin pulled Havyn closer to him, and then Severin's staff pressed against him. He closed his eyes and arched his hips. As Severin slowly filled him, Havyn panted through the pain. It did hurt, but not as much as he'd been expecting, but it wasn't entirely pleasurable either. Tears leaked out before he could help it. He hoped Severin wouldn't see them and stop. The pain wasn't just centred on where they were now joined, but at the base of his spine and in his abdomen too. Severin was just so big that Havyn wondered if he'd ever stretch that far at all. His erection had wilted somewhat and Havyn whimpered.

"Bear down around me," said Severin in a harsh whisper.

Havyn tried, he did, but the pain didn't seem to be diminishing at all. Severin took hold of Havyn's staff and stroked him back to full hardness which negated the pain a little, but not completely.

"Stroke yourself," said Severin. "Make yourself spill for me." Severin leaned down, kissing Havyn soundly, distracting Havyn from the burning stretch. Severin's kisses had always aroused him, and now was no exception. Havyn had never imagined it would feel like this. It hurt, yes, but he felt so connected to Severin. They belonged to each other now.

At last, Severin was fully sheathed inside him and he could feel every inch as Severin moved in and out of him. Soon they were rocking together in a rhythm as old as time itself. Havyn moaned and gasped while Severin made love to him. It was only pleasure Havyn felt now. He wanted them both to come. He frantically rubbed his staff, it was taking a bit longer than he expected, but the desire was still there.

Severin's thrusts were becoming more and more erratic. He had grabbed Havyn's hips and pounded into him so hard that the headboard was banging against the wall. Suddenly Severin stiffened and came. Havyn could feel the pulses of Severin's staff inside him when he climaxed. Havyn was disappointed that he hadn't come while Severin had been inside him, but knew there would be many more opportunities. He felt so close, so on edge, but hadn't quite reached his climax. Once Severin realised Havyn hadn't come yet, he pushed his hand between their bodies and stroked Havyn to one of the strongest orgasms he'd ever had. Havyn's toes curled in the sheets as he spurted jets of pearly white over Severin's hand and onto his own abdomen and chest.

"Ah! Sev'rin! Sev'rin!" Havyn shrieked as rope after rope left him and the world dwindled to white.

* * * *

Havyn groaned as he came around. His violet eyes were glazed with confusion.

"I fainted?" he asked.

Severin couldn't help the smile as he held out the glass of water for Havyn. "You did. It's very flattering actually. Did I hurt you?"

"It hurt a bit at first, but then it went away." Havyn sipped the water, and then he glanced down at his sticky body and grimaced. "I think I need a bath."

"You may have a bath on one condition."

"Oh? What's that?"

"You can have a bath if we share it."

Havyn's smile was blinding. "My dearest, Severin, I never intended anything else."

THE END

About the Author:

Annette Gisby grew up in a small town in Northern Ireland, moving to London when she was seventeen. Being a very small town there were no bookshops and a small library. When she'd devoured every book she could get her hands on in the library, she started writing her own stories so she would always have something to read later.

When not writing she enjoys reading, cinema, theatre, walks along deserted beaches or wandering around ruined castles (great places for inspiration!) New Zealand is her favourite place and she hopes to travel back there one day. She's a fan of Japanese Manga and Anime and one day hopes to learn Japanese.

She currently lives in Hampshire with her husband, a collection of porcelain dolls and stuffed penguins and enough books to fill a small library. It's diminishing gradually since the discovery of ebooks but still has a long way to go.

You can visit her website at www.annettegisby.n3.net

Other Books by the Author

Novels

Drowning Rapunzel
Silent Screams

Short Story Collection

Shadows of the Rose

Single Shorts

The Prince's Guard
Of Pets and Pleasures
The Witch Hunter

Non-Fiction

New Zealand with a Hobbit Botherer –
co-written with John Gisby

www.ingramcontent.com/pod-product-compliance
Lightning Source LLC
Chambersburg PA
CBHW061306280526
45784CB00002B/919